The Four Levers

How to Prepare for Retirement

Mike Kendra

To Heather

Contents

Note

This book is educational in nature and is the author's personal views. It is not investment advice, financial advice, or a recommendation. It is general information only and is not customized to any individual's circumstances. Any illustration of investment growth is hypothetical in nature; no such growth is guaranteed. In fact, you might lose money. You should seek the advice of a professional advisor before making any investment or financial planning decision or taking any action.

Part One
The History of Retirement

Introduction

Retire early! Spend more! Save less! Just kidding. If you are reading this book, it's unlikely you will be able to retire early, spend more, or save less than you are currently saving without making changes or "pulling levers" as indicated on the cover. In all likelihood, you will retire later, spend less and need to save more. And that's OK!

This book will be many things, but it will not be a magic wand or a road to riches. It will describe, in detail, specific actions people can take to get on track. In a world where most people only have $65,000 saved for retirement,[1] the reality is that it will most likely require action on your part to secure your financial future. It is never too late to begin to plan for retirement; however, the more time you have until retirement, the less drastic the action you may need to take will be. There will be no magic wand, but there will be a concrete set of steps anyone can take, regardless of age, present financial situation, and future goals.

One of the tallest roadblocks to people getting the financial advice, coaching, or planning they require is most people are shy, bashful, or embarrassed about their current situation. Meeting with a financial professional and revealing every last personal financial detail can be a very intimidating and downright scary experience. And to make matters worse, people are afraid of that same professional judging them, telling them they are not on track, or worse. But the truth is that a good financial advisor has seen it all, they won't judge you for how much you spend on liquor, Uber eats, streaming services and the like. Just remember, the past is the past and people can't change it. They can, however, plan for the future.

Many people conflate their financial assets with how well they have done in life. And if the average person has saved $65,000 for retirement, the average person probably needs some professional advice on planning for retirement. The people who need help the most are possibly the most intimidated. That's why it's smart to start getting help by simply reading this book; there is no one on the other side of the table judging you. You and I will never meet! Keep in mind that reading this book is only the first step; it is no substitute for professional advice from a financial advisor. But your money was not wasted! When you *do* meet with a financial advisor, you will be armed with a solid foundation of financial knowledge, questions to ask, and relief knowing that the right financial professional will help you without judging you.

Regardless of the complexity of your situation, the financial planning machine almost always simplifies down to pulling four levers: retirement age, day-to-day and monthly spending, retirement savings, and managing risk. The purpose of this book is to give you a working understanding of how the levers work, what levers are appropriate to pull based on various situations, and to help you take action. For any situation, there are actions you can take to improve your situation. No matter where you are in life, remember these two things: a) don't judge yourself and b) there is always an action you can take.

History of retirement.

Let's start off by defining retirement. What is retirement anyway? Like many things, people don't always agree on the definition. Retirement can mean a lot of things to different people. Let's agree on the following definition: Retirement means you no longer need to work at a job to cover your living expenses. Let's also agree that this is *a major goal* for a *major percentage of working people*. No matter how much a person loves working, most people would choose not to work if it was an option for them.

So... why do people work? People work because they need to earn money. Why do people need to earn money? So that they can afford basic necessities such as food and shelter, and also so they can do fun things such as travel and entertainment. Without money, these things would be very difficult.

So... if we need money to cover basics and extras, how can we ever stop working? There are a few overarching strategies this book will discuss. The main idea is to take advantage of ways to generate income that do not require work. Some of these ideas are very simple and straightforward. In fact, you are probably already a participant in one of them: Social Security. Some of these ideas are a little more complicated and take some explaining (and time to implement).

To summarize before we move forward, retirement means you no longer need to work at a job to cover your living expenses, and that is our goal! In this book, we'll explore together how to achieve it.

Where did the idea of retirement come from?

In the course of human history, retirement is a relatively new concept. Stipulated that there is no evidence *proving* humans 10,000 years ago worked up until death, can we agree the elder hunter-gatherers did not put aside enough meat, fruit, and veggies to move to Florida permanently? Retirement is new. Like, really new.

Over the course of human history, work has changed shape many times. Only since the Industrial Revolution have people worked in places that did not directly involve producing food. Practically speaking, people who produced food could not really store the food in any meaningful way. As long as there were hungry stomachs to feed, people had to work to produce food. There was no way to "save." In more modern times, people work, not to produce food directly, but to produce whatever their employer needs. Upon production of these goods or services, people are paid money, which is used to purchase the basic necessities such as food and shelter, and also the extras such as entertainment and leisure. Again, going back 200 or even 100 years, people produced enough to earn enough to cover the basics and maybe some of the extras, but there was no way to put aside resources or "save."

It's impossible to talk about retirement without talking about life expectancy. Life expectancy in the US was 76.1 years in 2021 according to the Centers for Disease Control and Prevention.[2] This number can be broken down in a variety of ways including race and sex. The 76.1 years figure is the life expectancy from birth, meaning the average of everyone who is born. A more realistic and relevant statistic is life expectancy at age 60, that is, how long can a 60-year-old expect to live? Life expectancy from birth includes data from all the people who (tragically) died young. Logically, people who have lived to age 60 are only concerned with their life expectancy going forward, not with the statistical likelihood of dying young due to various childhood ailments or situations. In a 2016 study, the findings revealed the life expectancy of a 60-year-old is 81 years.[3] For the sake of simplicity, let's agree the average life expectancy of anyone reading this book is 80, with male life expectancy being typically shorter and female life expectancy being typically longer.

Why is this important? If we are going to figure out what resources we need to sustain ourselves for the rest of our lives, then we are going to have to determine how long we expect to live. Granted, there is no practical way to determine precisely how long we will live, nor would we necessarily want to know, but we have to have a number upon which to base our plan. Retirement planning uses assumptions and statistical likelihoods. Assuming each person's life expectancy is 80, based on the data, let's consider being a little more conservative with our planning. If a healthy 60-year-old has a life expectancy of 80, then statistically speaking, there is probably a pretty good chance that person may live to 90. Age 90 is a very common age for planning purposes and is a good starting point for analysis.

Goals

It's also difficult to talk about retirement without talking about goals and goal setting. This is probably the first broken link in the chain from accepting your first job to buying that retirement condo in Sanibel Island. If you didn't *set* a goal to retire at X age, spending Y dollars per month, it's unlikely you are on track to *achieve* that goal. Do people get lucky? Yes! Do people work hard all their life, consistently underspend every month, look up at age 65 and find themselves in a great situation? Yes! Are there people who have saved well above the average of $65,000? Yes! Anything is possible, but those people probably either set professional goals that led to their financial success, or subconsciously set various retirement goals without explicitly setting time and dollar amounts.

Setting goals is the first step in making progress. Goal setting is a very simple concept that is very difficult to actually do. Because this is a book about retirement, we are going to talk about setting retirement goals. There are a wide variety of goals: personal fitness, health, finance, travel, education, family, and many others. We will focus on setting goals strictly for retirement.

When setting retirement goals, there are two main factors we will consider, one part is more *quantitative* and the other is more *qualitative*. First: how does one quantify retirement: what numbers do we need to understand and what calculations do we need to make?? We will need some support from financial planning software or at least an online calculator at a bare minimum. The second, and more importantly: how do you want *to feel* during retirement?

It will take careful consideration of both factors, and probably the help of a professional, to completely answer these questions. Getting into the numbers is not as difficult as it may first seem. To get a complete picture, which means an assessment of your current situation as well as projections into your financial future, the most robust option is to get professional help using financial planning software. This is a bit of work that is well worth the effort. After taking into consideration your current situation: financial assets, income, and expenses, the analysis will make projections into the future. This will give you a strong understanding of your retirement picture and future plans. For a less comprehensive analysis, you can consult with an online calculator.

Part of this analysis, particularly if you work with a professional, is to set your financial goals. While there are many considerations in the goal-setting process, the main consideration is answering the question: "How much do I need to spend each month?" Answering this question may or may not be a straightforward process.

The second question related to retirement goals: How do you want to feel during retirement? This feeling is based on your personal goals, family considerations, travel plans, volunteer goals, and how you enjoy spending your time. How will you fill your days from Monday to Friday, now that you do not need to spend the time working at your job? All these goals, activities, and aspirations will make you *feel* a certain way.

Here is another area where a professional financial advisor can help you navigate these waters. While your financial professional has not yet been "retired," they have helped dozens, hundreds, or possibly thousands of people transition to retirement. Your advisor will help you think of questions you may not think of on your own.

How do I know if I'm on track?

Whether you are one year away from retirement, or 30 years away from retirement, "doing the math" is not that hard. Before getting into the numbers, you will want to have a good understanding of what your goals are, and the more specific your goals are, the easier it is to assess your progress. After you have set your goal, your financial professional, or your online calculator, can give you an assessment of your current situation, project into your financial future, and tell you if you are on track. More importantly, if you are not on track, the analysis will give you ideas for what actions you can take to get on track.

Figuring out if you are on track is simple because "being on track" mathematically is a pretty simple exercise. There are a few ways to figure this out, but here is one:

1. Start with how much you wish to spend per year in retirement.
2. Subtract the income you are *guaranteed* to receive, such as Social Security or a pension.
3. Take this number and divide by your total retirement assets such as a 401(k), IRA, etc.
4. Take this number and multiply by 100 to get a percentage.

This is your *withdrawal rate*. Many articles have been written exploring the question, "What is a safe withdrawal rate?" Most people would say 2-4%. Some people would say 3-5%. Others say 2% is very conservative while 5% may be a little too aggressive. Can we agree on 4%? What does that mean? If you follow the steps above, and the result is 2-4%, congratulations, you have a very strong chance of sustaining that level of spending throughout retirement. If that number is more like 8-10%, you have a very strong chance of spending your assets too soon.

Here are two examples:

Sally and Sam

Total planned retirement expenses - $4,000 per month, or $48,000 per year

Sam's Social Security - $1,500 per month, or $18,000 per year

Sally's Social Security - $1,500 per month, or $18,000 per year

Total Guaranteed Income - $36,000 per year

Sam's IRA - $200,000

Sally's IRA - $200,000

Total Retirement Assets

So, let's use our four-step formula:

1. $48,000 per year in spending
2. $48,000 per year in spending minus $36,000 per year in Social Security equals $12,000
3. $12,000 divided by $400,000 equals .03
4. .03 times 100 = 3%

Right in the sweet spot. Nice job, Sam and Sally!

Let's look at Sam and Sally's neighbors, Joe and Jessie.

Total planned retirement expenses - $6,000 per month, or $72,000 per year

Joe's Social Security - $1,600 per month, or $19,20 per year

Jessie's Social Security - $1,600 per month, or $19,200 per year

Jessie's pension - $500 per month, or $6,000 per year

Total Guaranteed Income - $44,400

Joe's IRA - $150,000

Jessie's 401(k)- $150,000

Total Retirement Assets: $300,000

So, let's use our four-step formula:

1. $72,000 per year in spending
2. $72,000 per year in spending minus $44,400 per year in Social Security equals $27,600
3. $27,600 divided by $300,000 equals .092
4. .092 times 100 = 9.2%

This may or may not work for Joe and Jessie. The odds are pretty good they will outlive their money.

I'm on track. Now what?

You've set your goals, you've done the analysis, and it looks like...you are on track! Congratulations, that is great news! You should be proud of your accomplishments. So now what? Keep doing what you have been doing. Whatever you have been doing is working, so keep going. Keep meeting with your financial professional, they will keep you on track. Each year or so, you may have changes and updates to your situation that warrant checking in on your financial plan. Doing this on an annual basis will keep you on track. This is the same idea as going to the dentist every 6-12 months. You make the dentist aware of any changes to your situation, and the dentist does a routine checkup to make sure everything is OK.

I'm not on track. Now what?

You are not alone! Keep reading!

Part Two
The Four Levers

Amazon reveals over 10,000 books on personal finance (boy, am I glad you found this one!). Google search yields 2 billion websites on personal finance. You could spend the next decade reading every book, website, and article with questionable results. The main goal here is to distill a wide-ranging and complex topic into a few key concepts.

If we think about our retirement analysis as a machine, like many machines, there are knobs and levers to move when you want to make adjustments to how the machine is running. There are no perfect analogies, but a task of similar complexity is flying an airplane. An airplane, while moving 400 miles per hour at about 35,000 feet, moves on three axes. These axes are *pitch, yaw, and roll*. Pitch is when the pilot pulls the nose up to take off. Yaw is when the pilot turns the plane right or left without moving up or down. And roll is when the pilot makes the plane bank to one side or the other. What makes a pilot a pilot is the ability to move on all three axes *at the same time!*

To control the plane over these three axes, the pilot uses three separate controls. The pilot changes the *elevators,* typically located in the tail, to control the pitch. The pilot uses the *rudder* to change the yaw, and the *ailerons* to change the roll.[4] He or she is controlling these three levers at the same time, while going 150-400 miles per hour. Be sure to thank your pilot after your next flight.

Flying and retiring are two different things, obviously. But hopefully you get the idea that pulling a lever at one point in time is going to have an impact on your machine at another point in time. In flying, the time between pulling a lever and moving the plane is typically very short (seconds to minutes), while in retirement planning, you might pull a lever today that does not make an impact for two, ten, or twenty years.

When it comes to retirement, there are only four levers we are going to pull. These four levers control the four main inputs for any retirement analysis:

- Retirement Age: When are you going to retire?
- Monthly Spending: How much are you going to spend when you retire?
- Accumulating Assets: How much are you saving for retirement right now?
- Managing Risk: Am I taking the appropriate amount of risk with my retirement investments?

As part of setting our retirement goals, you already had to answer these questions, at least partially. And as part of the analysis to answer the question, "Am I on track for my retirement goal?", the answers to these questions were fed into the retirement machine, along with your current situation. And if it turns out you are "not on track," all we are going to do is change the answers to these questions. Or pull these levers. It really is that simple! Simple, but not necessarily easy because change can be difficult for people and a lot of these resolutions come down to making personal change.

If you have read this far, you are probably not on track for retirement. And that's OK! And as mentioned in the title, there are terms and conditions that apply. Well, these are the terms and conditions. The four main areas to focus on are: when you retire, how much you will spend in retirement, how much you are currently saving for retirement, and how much risk you're taking. The good news is that there are only four of them, and the better news is that it is not difficult to make improvements on these areas. The less-good news is that the less time you have until your retirement goal, the more drastic the changes you need to make will be. And that's still OK!

Over the next several chapters, we are going to break down each of the four areas or "levers." Pulling these levers, or taking specific action in these four areas, will impact your goal of fully retiring.

The first lever we are going to pull is: when do you want to retire? Do you want to retire tomorrow, next year, 10 years from now, or 30 years from now? Answering this question will make a significant difference in the potential outcomes, mainly due to the Time Value of Money, a topic we'll discuss later in the book. The bottom line is that the sooner you wish to retire, the more resources you will need, all other levers being equal.

Once we know when we are going to retire, the next lever we are going to pull is: how much do you plan on spending per year in retirement? Or depending on how you budget your spending, how much do you plan on spending per month in retirement? A common answer to this question is: as much as possible! That is understandable, and not entirely crazy. There are many ways to think about spending, control spending, and optimize spending throughout a long, successful retirement.

We've established when we are going to retire and how much we wish to spend per year or per month in retirement. The third lever to pull is: how much are you currently saving for retirement? The answers to the first two questions are somewhat subjective and partially informed by your dreams. The answer to the third question is a cold, hard fact. Now is not the time to lie to yourself or make excuses. Perhaps the answer is: I am not saving anything. And that's OK!

The final lever to pull is: are you taking an appropriate level of risk with your retirement investments? If the first two answers are based on dreams, and the third answer is based on fact, the fourth answer is complicated! The following answers are completely acceptable:

- I have no idea.
- What is an appropriate level of risk?
- Yes!
- No.
- Please help.

Now we have taken a quick tour of the levers we are going to pull to adjust our retirement plans. Once we understand what the levers are and how they work, next we need to understand Archimedes' quote, "Give me a lever long enough, and a fulcrum on which to place it, and I shall move the world." What was he talking about?

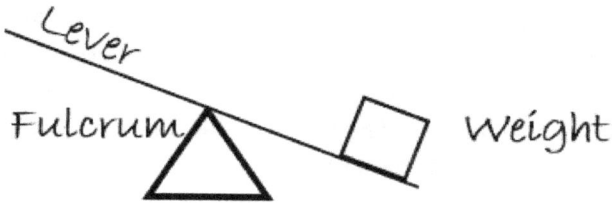

The principle he was describing is: The longer the lever, the easier it is to move the weight.

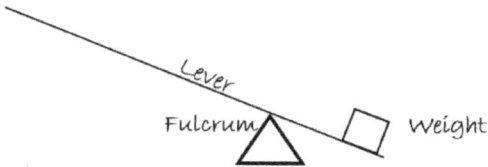

A longer lever means less force required to lift the same weight

And in theory, a long enough lever can lift the world. It may not be practical, but the math works.

Now, how does this relate to our four levers for retirement? In the case of retirement planning, the length of the lever is the amount of *time* you have until retirement. All other levers being equal, the longer we have until our retirement goal, the longer is our lever. And the longer our lever, the easier it is to lift the load.

Why is it easier to lift the load? There are many reasons, and the main reason is the time value of money. There are countless books, articles, and videos about the time value of money. Another way to phrase this is "the power of compound interest." The main idea is when we invest our money, it will grow over time. Mainly due to the growth of our investments, plus any interest or dividends we receive. Over time, as you add to these investments, your growth, interest, and dividends will begin to receive *growth, interest, and dividends.* Now your money is making money! It starts slowly at first, but over 5, 10, 20, or 30 years, the growth can become exponential. So, the longer our time horizon, the longer time our investments have to grow.

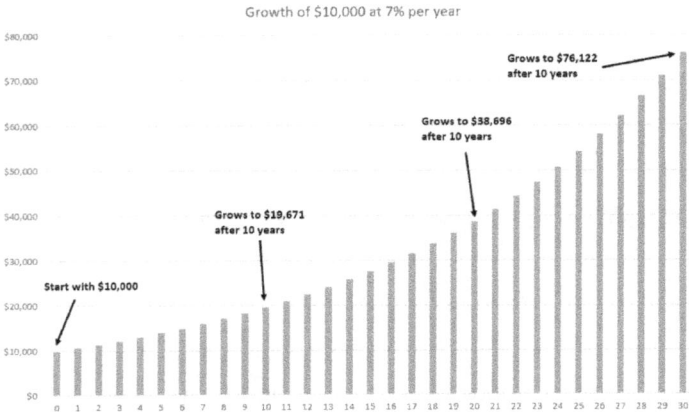

Growth of $10,000 at 7% per year

Grows to $76,122 after 10 years

Grows to $38,696 after 10 years

Grows to $19,671 after 10 years

Start with $10,000

Note: this chart illustrates the hypothetical growth of $10,000 at a 7% annual return. No one is guaranteed these results.

Well, what if we don't have a lot of time until retirement? That's OK! If we go back to our lever and fulcrum analogy, the more time we have, the easier the load will be. But regardless of how much or little time you have until retirement, there are always levers to pull. The load may be heavy or light, but there is always a solution. The rest of the book will be a "deep dive" into the four areas, how they impact your plans, and how you move these levers in your personal financial life.

Chapter 1
The First Lever: Retirement Age

Dani and Deb Delay Days with Grandkids

Meet Dani and Deb. Dani and Deb are young Baby Boomers. Dani is about to turn 59 and Deb just turned 60. Deb and Dani met a little later in life and got married around age 40. They both grew up in New York and currently live outside of Washington D.C. Deb has two children from a previous marriage and looks forward to spending more time with her three grandchildren, who live in the next town over.

Dani has worked for the Federal Government for the past 30 years as an accountant. Dani loves the significance of the work and the number-crunching the job entails. Deb has always had a passion for helping those less fortunate and has worked with the same non-profit organization as operations manager for the last 5 years. Dani loves the work of an accountant yet feels like it's time to move on. Serving the country while gaining deep expertise in an area is incredibly rewarding, but after 30 years, the work has become routine for Dani. Deb is a lot more energized by the work in a non-profit organization. There is never a dull moment and there are always new projects to work on.

Since they married later in life, they always talked about retiring relatively early so they could enjoy a long retirement together. After 5 years in her current role, Deb is just getting into a good groove and making major improvements. But, because Dani is ready to move on, they both agreed to explore an early retirement.

They read online that people can start their Social Security at age 62, so they figured this might be a good place to start retirement. Since Deb is about a year older than Dani, they agreed to consider retirement when Deb is 63 and Dani is 62. Between the two of them, saving for retirement has never been a major priority and they have minimal savings set aside for retirement. What they do have is three main sources of retirement income: Dani's Social Security, Deb's Social Security, and Dani's pension from the Federal Government.

While these three sources of income are significant when compared to their current incomes, their total retirement income when these pensions start would be less than their current level of spending. After meeting with their advisor, they came to the following conclusions about the retirement levers: pulling the savings lever won't help all that much – they are only a few years away from retirement. But, if they were to pull the spending lever and reduce their planned retirement spending or pull the retirement age lever and delay their retirement, they would be able to cover their spending with their retirement income. Decreasing their spending did not appeal to them. Dani and Deb feel they do not live a very extravagant lifestyle. They cover their basics every month, live in a comfortable home, and take one or two nice vacations per year. That's it. When they looked at what they were spending, they felt that reducing their spending was not really possible and not something they were willing to do.

What they *were* willing to do was continue to work for a few more years. In Dani's case especially, every year retirement is delayed, the federal pension increases. And for both Dani and Deb, each year retirement is delayed, they both increase their Social Security. The answer to the next question is a straightforward math problem: how long do they need to delay their retirement so that their pensions increase to the point of covering their spending? This is something their financial advisor could easily help with.

In their case, it turned out that working five more years would put them in a much better position for retirement. This is only two years beyond their original retirement plan. Dani and Deb discussed it and how it made them feel. Deb had no hesitations regarding an additional two years of working. Five more years in Deb's current role would help her organization tremendously and put it in a strong position for the future. It took a little more thought and reflection on Dani's part. While the work is interesting, 30 years is a long time to do anything. The thought of an additional two years was not Dani's dream situation, but understanding the reasoning behind the delay was critical to the decision. Dani sees the wisdom in optimizing the federal pension and is appreciative of the opportunity to make this type of decision that is in her best interest. In the meantime, they will look forward to more time with Deb's grandchildren.

Pulling the retirement age lever

The first lever we are going to explore in detail is retirement age. More specifically, we need to answer the question: when are you retiring? This is an important question! Here are some common answers:

- It depends on when my spouse retires.
- When I reach Social Security full retirement age.
- When I am eligible for Medicare.
- When my pension begins.
- I have no idea.

Any of these answers are a perfectly fine place to start when thinking about when you will want to retire. Retirement is an emotional event. Before you get into the *when* of retirement, try considering *why you are retiring in the first place*. Once you have thought about and understand *why* you are retiring, it may be much easier to determine *when*.

You may also want to engage others in helping to determine when you are going to retire. If you are married, your spouse may have some input. Your financial advisor may have some input. Your tax professional may have some input. Your recently retired friends may have some input. The more people with whom you talk this through, the more confident you'll feel about your decision.

For most people, setting a retirement goal means planning on a certain age for retirement. Maybe you have a goal to retire at 65, because that's what your parents did. Or maybe you wish to wait until your Social Security full retirement age, which is probably 67. Or maybe you have a defined benefit pension plan waiting for you (congratulations, by the way). These are all common ways to decide on when to retire.

Once you decide on when, then your retirement plan will revolve around this milestone. And like we learned in the first chapter, you may or may not be on track to retire at this age.

And that's OK! Let's assume that you are not on track to retire at this age. You would like to stop working, but the financial situation does not yet allow for it. Not ideal, but you simply keep working at your current job.

There are many options available to delay your retirement in a manner that best suits you.

The first and obvious option is you just keep working. You currently have a job, that's why you want to retire. Maybe you like your job, maybe you hate your job. The reality is: the situation works. You add value to your employer, they compensate you in some mutually agreeable way. Your income covers your spending, mortgage, taxes, whatever is happening in your life.

Perhaps if you don't want to continue working at your current job, let's explore some variations on continuing to work, albeit in a different situation. Fair warning: these options all involve varying degrees of risk. If you are the type of person who does not like risk and the possibility of failure, perhaps the best course of action is to continue at your current employer.

Some people are just plain lucky. They find a job they love doing. Whatever it is about the job — the hours, the people, the location, the nature of the work — they truly enjoy doing it and it is something they can continue doing for an extended period of time. Well, if this is your situation, you are playing a strong hand. You can continue working, regardless of your retirement plans. And if you truly love working, large portions of this book will be completely irrelevant!

If you enjoy parts of your employment but are looking to increase your overall enjoyment, reducing the overall time spent working, or changing how you work, perhaps there is an opportunity to translate into a consulting role. Depending on your skillset, there may be a high demand applying your skills to specific problems, without engaging in full-time employment. Consulting can be a win-win on several fronts. The hiring company does not necessarily want to employ someone 40 hours per week, with the salary, vacation time, payroll taxes, benefits, and the like. It may be easier for them to find someone to engage in a specific project and pay the bill for the project. Then, when the engagement is over, they no longer have to carry the cost of an employee.

This can be a win for the consultant as well because you may be able to charge a higher hourly rate, define the exact scope of the engagement, and clearly define when you are available (and when you are not available). Once the project is done, you can take time off, or begin to look for the next project. Depending on how in-demand your skills are, you might find the next project before you even complete the current project. Books have been written on starting a consulting business, so do your own research on getting this started. Regardless of your career path, understand that it is a very viable option for many people.

Another approach people take is to find a second career. Perhaps there are some skills in your toolkit that translate over to another career. Or perhaps you are looking to make a wholesale change in your employment. Some people work an entire career in a field, only to find themselves bored and unchallenged with the situation yet not ready to fully retire.

A somewhat uncommon, but noble and challenging path is to become an educator. Education systems across the country are constantly seeking out new talent to fill classroom education ranks.[5] There is an acute need in any technical field, so if you have these types of skills, this would be a great second career for 3 to 15 years. Again, this would be another win-win. The education system you join gets an educator with many years of practical, hands-on experience while the new educator will gain meaningful, challenging employment and a steady income.

If you don't want to take on the challenging environment of education, another path would be to find something "easy." "Easy" work means different things to different people, so regardless of how challenging you perceive your work to be, you can always find something "easy." Maybe that means less time, less responsibility, less stress, or less thinking.

There are infinite possibilities to finding work that is easier than your current situation. It might make sense to you to work on a part-time basis, where you can work enough to earn your desired income, without the stress and responsibility of a full-time position.

Another common approach is to find an employer who offers health benefits. Most employers require employees to work full-time in order to receive full benefits, but there are some larger employers who will allow you to enroll in the company benefits program even if you are only a part-time employee. The main reason to do this is to access a health insurance plan that might otherwise be very expensive. Typically, employer-sponsored health insurance plans are very cost-effective, due to having a larger employee base on which to negotiate insurance pricing. This plan will almost always be lower in cost than a private medical insurance plan.

One primary use of this strategy is to use these company health benefits as a bridge to Medicare. Many people find themselves in their early 60s, ready to move on from their full-time career, but not yet ready, emotionally and/or financially, to fully retire. This is a nice transition that allows you to earn some income, and continue receiving cost-effective benefits, while slightly delaying your retirement.

With the explosive growth of social media (Facebook, Youtube, Instagram, Twitter, etc.) over the last 10-plus years, there are now infinite ways to generate income using these platforms. This is another area where books have been written on strategies, tactics, and tips for engaging in social media.

There are a few key things to understand. The main point to realize is we live in a content-driven, attention-driven economy. When compared to traditional media platforms from 50, or 30, or even 15 years ago, the demand for content today is exponentially higher. 30 years ago, there were only so many television networks and so many movie studios. Without a doubt, it was a very large number, and the demand was high, yet it was a fixed number. It was by no means infinite.

Today's demand for content is essentially infinite. If you take the media landscape of 20 years ago, and now add all the social media, as well as the "non-traditional" media such as Netflix, Hulu, Amazon, and many others, these publishers of content have a lot of time to fill up!

As someone with experience, you could create a couple different types of content that would be unique to you. First, you could create content around a hobby you are passionate about. You could review products, explain how to enter the hobby, or make frequent videos about your adventures. The second technique would be giving advice based on your specific skillset. People who are new to your industry are always looking for opportunities to learn. And in a work-world that is much more "remote," the opportunity for coaching and mentorship is not always present. You could become an online mentor for people in your industry. The more niche, the better.[6]

The last idea we'll discuss is the hardest to do, but it could potentially be the most rewarding. You could start a business. This is much, much easier said than done. But the possibilities are infinite. Out of the infinite possibilities, you might consider filtering them down to: something you have experience in, a business that does not take up a lot of time, and a business that does not take a lot of capital. Remember, the goal is to transition to a phase of working *less* and preserving some of your money, so it's probably not best to start a business that will take up 40, 50, or 60 hours per week while draining your financial resources.

Starting a business based on what you have experience in may or may not make sense for you. And it may sound a lot like the consulting business discussed earlier. But maybe you work in a field where a competitor could easily enter, or maybe you have operations skills from one career that would translate over to a simpler small business. In any event, starting a small business, especially one that you could turn over to someone to keep running for you, is a nice way to generate supplemental income in retirement.

Again, being mindful you do not want to commit to something that will take up the majority of your week, consider seeking a business that would require limited hours. There are all kinds of businesses that are open limited hours, for whatever reason, be it a coffee shop, a lemonade stand, or music lessons. I'm not suggesting any of those for you specifically — they're simply examples to get your wheels turning. Alternatively, you could consider a seasonal business. Maybe you wish to travel one part of the year and work in a different part of the year. You don't need to be extremely creative or inventive to brainstorm a dozen seasonal business ideas.

The last, and most important consideration for starting a small business is finding something that does not require significant cash to start up. Remember, you are doing this to earn income and preserve the assets you have. Let's say you have $500,000 saved up for retirement and are considering delaying retirement for a few years. Well, the last thing you want to do is put $200,000 into a Subway franchise, a dry-cleaning business, or a new restaurant. Think light and nimble!

Let's review the first lever. The first lever we can pull, in the event we are slightly off course for retirement, is to adjust *retirement age*. In other words, *retire later*. There are many ways to retire later and we discussed a handful of them. On one end of the spectrum, you just keep doing what you are doing, for as long as you can keep doing it. Maybe you love your job, or maybe you love spending money. Either way, continuing to work will help "the math." On the other end of the spectrum, you can dabble in as light of a work schedule as you desire, while keeping in mind the purpose of continuing to work. Maybe you are continuing to work for strictly financial reasons, and the income you earn helps with "the math." Or maybe you are continuing for emotional reasons — you are not yet ready to fully retire and wish to remain engaged and productive in a new endeavor. Regardless of the reason, keep in mind the reason why you continue to work and understand the exact financial impact this decision has on your potential retirement. Three more levers to go!

Chapter 2
The Second Lever – Retirement spending

Ronnie and Rick reduce their monthly spending

Meet Ronnie and Rick, who are also from the Baby Boomer generation. Rick runs a coffee shop outside of Houston and will turn 66 this year. Ronnie, who just turned 65, is a mechanical engineer at a small manufacturing plant in Houston, TX. While Ronnie has a brilliant mind, his body is starting to show some signs of wear and tear. Ronnie and Rick each love their job and would continue working for many more years, but Ronnie's deteriorating health is starting to become a concern. They originally planned on working until at least 70, but now they think it might be best to retire next year.

Ronnie and Rick like to work hard and play hard. They've never said "no" to a good time, but early on, they both decided they would play hard *after* saving for retirement. Ronnie has been at the same plant for the last 10 years, and before that, he worked for a large manufacturer right out of college. Ronnie enrolled in the 401(k) about 30 years ago and diligently saved 10% of his salary every month. "Set it and forget it" is what a co-worker told Ronnie all those years ago. And "forget it" Ronnie did. A couple of years ago, Ronnie was floored when he checked his online account to find $575,000 in his 401(k). There were many highs and lows over the years, but sticking with the market all those years (decades!) paid off.

Rick is also no stranger to savings. Rick worked in a variety of jobs over the years and most recently, the coffee shop has been doing quite well. So well, in fact, Rick has been able to contribute to a retirement plan for all the shop's employees. As a result of saving for the past 10 or so years, Rick has been able to accumulate $250,000 in a tax-deferred account. Between Ronnie and Rick's retirement savings, they have a solid nest egg to fund their retirement.

In addition to retirement assets, they each have Social Security benefits to rely on. Because they are both past the earliest retirement age, they each could retire tomorrow and begin collecting benefits. That, however, was not the plan. They each enjoy their work and planned on working until 70. But Ronnie hasn't been feeling well lately. The job is stressful and they keep a pretty active social life. Multiple doctors insist there is nothing wrong, but that it is simply time to *slow down*. The stress and strain on Ronnie have bled over into the workplace. Ronnie has made some mistakes lately, which is out of character, and it's starting to have a negative impact.

They decided it was time to meet with a financial planner to see what their retirement could look like. As an engineer, Ronnie is comfortable with numbers, but feels overwhelmed when it comes to their financial situation. After several conversations and some hard work, Ronnie, Rick, and the financial planner determined that they would not be able to sustain what they are currently spending throughout retirement. Ronnie and Rick each have a pretty high salary and they are used to a certain lifestyle. And while they have pretty significant assets saved for retirement – over $825,000 between them – the retirement assets plus Social Security is not enough to fund their current lifestyle indefinitely. Given Ronnie's health, they don't want to pull the retirement age lever (the first lever) and retire later – they want to retire now! And if they want to retire now, they won't be able to pull the retirement savings lever (the third lever — we'll explore that next!) and save more for retirement. And there is not much they can do with taking more risk (the fourth lever — more on that soon!); the financial planner already agreed they are invested appropriately in a mix of stock and bond mutual funds. That leaves the spending lever. If they want to retire now, they'll have to reduce their spending. How much? That's a simple math problem the financial planner can quickly solve. In this case, they had to reduce their spending by about 15%. While it's not the end of the world, it's a significant amount for them. They have some difficult decisions to make about where to spend the money, but it made them feel great they could retire at the end of the year.

Pulling the retirement spending lever

The second, and probably the least popular lever, has to do with how much money you will spend every month. Why every month? Most people manage their spending on a monthly basis. Maybe you are currently paid on a weekly basis or a bi-weekly basis. Maybe you have some other way of keeping track of your spending. What most people find is managing your spending on a monthly basis is the easiest way to manage it in retirement. Your Social Security will be paid monthly, a pension or annuity will be paid monthly; and conversely, you may still have a monthly mortgage or other monthly bills. So managing on a monthly basis is probably the simplest thing to do.

If you are going to manage your spending on a monthly basis, it is very important to understand how much that spending is. Before we cover spending in all its glory, let's remember a couple of things. First, we don't need to judge ourselves on how much money we are currently spending or how much we wish to spend in the future. And second, at least initially, the most important part of spending is not to worry about spending too much or too little but to understand simply *what* you are spending in the first place.

The first step toward controlling your spending is to understand where all your money goes each month. To figure this out, it's very helpful to understand the difference between *gross income* and *net income*. Gross income is the full amount you are paid, whether it comes from a job where you work or a retirement benefit you collect. If you negotiated a salary of $75,000 per year, that's your gross income. Or if your Social Security is $1,800 per month, that's your gross benefit. To arrive at your net income, there are various things taken out of your pay. Specifically, we are talking about taxes. Federal, state, Social Security, and Medicare are the typical taxes withheld from people's paycheck.

From here, you will arrive at your net income, which is the amount actually deposited into your account. This is the amount of money you must use until the next time you are paid. Here, we have arrived at the simplest way of determining your monthly spending: simply figure out your *net income* on a monthly basis. This is what you must spend — no more and no less.

Taking things one step further, if you find yourself putting items on a credit card without paying off the credit card each month, this is called "carrying a balance," you are probably spending *more* than your net income. And conversely, if you find yourself building up money in your checking account each month, you are probably spending *less* than your income. At this point, no one is judging, it's important to understand exactly what is happening each month. You won't be able to take actions to improve this situation without knowing exactly what you are doing.

There is another more detailed way to understand your spending. This is the dreaded "B" word. Budget. Budgets are no fun. Budgets are for boring people, right? Wrong! Budgeting is simply a tool. Budgets will allow you to go into more detail on where your spending goes each month. There are plenty of tools online to help you budget.[7]

The goal is to identify all the areas in which you spend money each month. Cable, phones, internet, food, dining out, gas, car insurance, you name it. Then assign an amount to each of those categories. This is not a place to "fudge the numbers." If you spend $200 per month on beer, this is the time to identify it. Personally, my wife spends about $100 per month at TJ Maxx on who knows what, so that's a line item. There are also smartphone apps that can help with this process.

Once you have the full list with an amount for each item, all you need to do is add up the total. If you are completing this online or in a good, old-fashioned spreadsheet, the math becomes pretty easy. Now you have a grand total of what you probably spend each month. From here, you can compare this total to your true net income. If your budget is less than your net income, that's great. And if your budget is more than your net income, that's OK too, at least now you are aware you're probably spending more than your income allows and you can begin to take actions to improve the situation.

One key benefit of using the budgeting technique is now you have a complete listing of all your spending. And if you find yourself in the situation where your spending is more than your income, now you know exactly where your money is going, unless you lied to yourself! With a complete list of spending, you can identify areas that don't seem right. Maybe you are overspending in some areas which could easily be reduced.

The other key benefit of using a budget is allowing you to see where your money is going, so you can make sure it aligns with your values and priorities in life. This is a great time to have a conversation about the things that are important to you as a person. If you've already thought this through, great! Now you can make sure you are spending your money in accordance with your values. And if you haven't thought about your values, there are plenty of online tools to help you think through them and identify what are the top three-to-five things you value most in life. Once you identify your values, then you can begin to prioritize your spending in accordance with your values.

And after establishing first where the money is being spent and then how much is being spent, ultimately there comes a decision point about what the spending amount *should* be each month. This is the number that must be managed on a monthly basis. Practically everyone, except the top 1% of the top 1% of wealthy people, has a number that must be managed on a monthly basis. This is neither good nor bad, it is simply a mathematical and financial fact.

The go-go years, the slow-go years, and the no-go years

You and your financial advisor, if you are working with one, are going to spend a lot of time talking about how much you plan on spending in retirement. This is very important for two reasons: first, this spending number is the main input to your retirement calculations. Whether you are working with a professional, using an online calculator, or giving it your best shot in Excel, this is a key number to know. The second and most important reason is the amount you plan on spending in retirement is emotional. Furthermore, the more your lifestyle changes, the more emotional it may become. The amount you can spend will roughly determine your lifestyle. If the amount you are able to spend in retirement is roughly in line with your current spending, and thus your current lifestyle, this number may not have much emotion attached to it. But should you find yourself in a situation where you need to reduce your spending in retirement, that may not feel so great. Especially when you consider what you will have to give up in order to reduce your spending. Looking at a report showing you have to reduce your spending by $1,000 per month may not feel like anything, but once you face the pressure of deciding where that $1,000 per month will come from, emotions may take flight. Golf less? Dine out less? Travel less? That's emotional!

This is not all doom and gloom, even if you have to reduce your lifestyle in retirement. Here is where we need to understand the distinction between the lifestyle you're going to live in retirement "go-go" years versus the lifestyle you're going to live in the "slow-go" and "no-go" years. This is an important distinction and we need to revisit our discussion about life expectancy.

The "go-go" years. Early in retirement, particularly in the first few years, you will experience a string of roughly 500 to 5,000 Saturdays. In. A. Row. Think about it: your last day of work was for all practical purposes, The Mother of All Fridays. You punched out at 5pm. You went out to dinner or some party. Maybe you partied all night, or maybe you went home and went to bed. Either way, you woke up the next morning and it was Saturday. You have no work and you have some money in the bank. What are you going to do? Whatever you want! So, you have yourself a "nice little Saturday." Then you wake up the next morning, and it's Saturday again.

This might sound great, but here's the problem. You have *no work responsibilities*, and therefore, you have infinite time to do stuff. Since you have no responsibilities, you have no work income coming in. And because you have infinite time to do stuff, you are going to spend more money. While there are some hobbies that are free, I challenge you to go an entire weekend without spending money. You may have chores, housework, errands, exercise, hobbies. Sure. But what else? You go to the coffee shop for a coffee and a bagel. You stop by the paint store to pick up a gallon of paint. Maybe you take your grandkids to the zoo. And of course, you go out for dinner somewhere. This is the main difference between a string of Saturdays and working a full-time job. At the job, you are fully occupied with your job duties; and in exchange for your services, someone is paying you. You are keeping busy *and* bringing money into the household. Economically speaking, this string of Saturdays is the polar opposite.

And let's not forget, this string of never-ending Saturdays is what will become known as "normal life." And when we need a break from "normal life." what do we do? We go on vacation! That means that on top of the stream of Saturdays, you will continue to go on vacation. In fact, your vacations will probably be supercharged for a few different reasons. First, remember if you only have Saturdays in your life; you don't need to end your vacation to return to work. Heading to Florida? Why only go for a week? Why not 10 days? Why not 3 weeks? And the second difference is: Many people are going to want to start tackling the Bucket List trips. If you live in New England, going to the Cape is great. And if you've been going there your entire life, perhaps there is somewhere a little more far-flung you would like to visit. Portugal? Australia? Swiss Alps? Great, and probably more expensive. Therefore, on top of the spending in "normal life," you probably also want to account for additional travel.

Again, none of this is a problem. Unless we don't plan for it. This is where our "planned amount of retirement spending — aka our budget" will become critical. We need to be realistic about how much we can and/or will spend. And we need to be accurate because this string of Saturdays will go on for as long as you are healthy, or until you run out of money, whichever comes first.

The "slow-go" years. This brings us to the next phase of retirement, the point at which you begin to slow things down. Maybe this phase is more like a long string of Sundays. Now we are going to transition to a period where we are simply going to do less. And doing less, generally, will cost less money. Just like a Sunday. How are Sundays different from Saturdays? Maybe on a Sunday, you practice your faith, you visit with family, you cook a large meal at home, or sit by the fire and read a book. Just as Saturdays have a distinct feel to them, Sundays do as well. And what do all these Sunday activities have in common? They are all free or inexpensive. Maybe you still grab that coffee on a Sunday, or maybe you go out for lunch. But overall, you will spend less money. Why does this matter? It matters because our retirement spending is going impact our financial calculations. And how we feel.

This might be the phase in life where our health starts to go downhill. Not drastically, of course, but over time, you start to move a little bit slower. Maybe you aren't so keen on boarding a plane for a 10-hour flight to an African safari. Maybe your grandkids are driving to your house to visit *you*, instead of you picking them up for a trip to Disney. Life just starts to slowwwwww downnnnnnnnnnnn. And this is OK.

The "no-go" years. Let's be candid; life happens in cycles, and we are going to start addressing the later stages in the cycle of life. To put it another way, in the four seasons of life, everyone (except those who die young) must enter winter. You can read all sorts of books about the aging process, whether you are considering aging through the lens of health and wellness, psychology, spirituality, or religion. One common message those thousands of books convey is: We are all going to die. If you are disappointed, you'll have to take this up with your higher power as this is well above my pay grade.

Continuing our Day of The Week metaphor, if our early retirement is a series of Saturdays, and our middle retirement is a long line of lazy Sundays, the last phase of retirement is probably more like Mondays...with a doctor's appointment. A lot of doctor's appointments. You don't have to go to work, but you do have to go to Doctor A at 10am, then Doctor B at 2pm...and then two weeks later, there's a follow up. Maybe there's bloodwork. And another follow-up. And so on and so forth. Nothing crazy, nothing too taxing. But it takes up time *and* after all these appointments, you don't necessarily have the energy to fly to Vegas for a 48-hour poker bender.

This is where our analogy becomes far from perfect, mainly due to the potential variation in your spending level. On the one hand, your spending will definitely decrease. Depending on your health level, you may not have the inclination to travel abroad, paint your house, go out to dinner four nights a week, or add that deck to your backyard. Your discretionary spending will most certainly decrease. On the flip side, again depending on your health level, there is a significant risk you may incur substantial healthcare costs.

The prudent financial planner, or prudent individual if you are working alone, will consider medical and long-term care costs in retirement planning. There are later chapters devoted to this topic, so for now, let's separate out planning for *potential* medical and long-term care costs versus planning for lifestyle spending. Regardless of the medical and long-term care costs, your discretionary spending will most certainly decrease.

JP Morgan retirement spending study

It's fine if you don't believe everything I'm telling you. In fact, don't take my word for it! There are all kinds of reports about retirement spending.

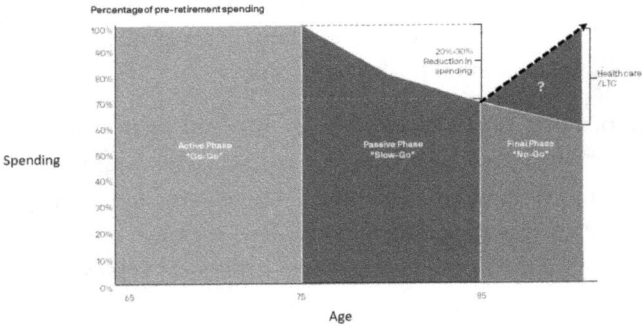

Percentage of pre-retirement spending

Spending / Age

Source: The Prosperous Retirement: Guide to the New Reality, Michael K. Stein, CFP, TRW, pp. 9–18

This chart[8], in one nice, neat graphic, fully supports the previous section. On the horizontal axis, or X-axis for all you algebra teachers out there, you will find people's age. On the vertical axis, or Y-axis, you will see the spending level.

You may have read the previous section and thought, "This is totally wrong; what about medical costs?" This is a fair point and cannot be discounted. If you go back to the chart in that section, and look closer, you will notice that while the trend of overall spending goes down, medical spending actually increases. This can make planning very difficult.

Let's examine the types of medical expenses people really encounter. We can group them into premiums, deductibles, and out-of-pocket expenses. The good news is that a large portion of typical, routine medical expenses are covered by Medicare. The vast majority of people age 65 and over rely on

Medicare for their primary medical coverage. Medicare covers basic medical issues such as hospital stays, routine medical visits, preventative care, and prescriptions. There are several components that make up what we call Medicare: Part A is no cost "hospital insurance"; Part B is relatively low-cost health insurance; and Part D covers prescriptions at a relatively low cost. In 2023, it's prudent to budget $200-$300 per person per month for Medicare.

Beyond the basic health and medical coverage, there are countless options. A popular strategy is to pair Medicare, which is essentially a government-administered health program, with a private policy. These policies are often called "Medigap" or "Medicare Supplement." They can cost between $100 and $500 per month per person and cover supplemental items such as specialty doctor visits as well as copays.

The Medicare plus supplement package, regardless of what supplement is chosen, is pretty standard for most people and is relatively straightforward for financial planning. On the low end, it may cost $300 per person per month, and on the high end, it may cost $800 per person per month. This is where the simplicity ends: with two potential outcomes that are difficult for planning. First, maybe a person has a serious issue that is not covered by Medicare. Either the treatment takes so long or is so expensive, it goes beyond the scope of Medicare. Or perhaps the medical issue occurs before Medicare age. Either way, there are a good number of medical issues that can cost significant money that must be paid "out of pocket." This is why, while the typical retirement medical may cost only $300 per month, it may be prudent to plan on a much more significant amount, like $1,000 to $1,500 per month. Taking this level of spending into account will ensure a significant portion of retirement assets are earmarked for future potential issues.

Pulling the second lever – adjusting retirement spending to *spend less* – is arguably the least fun of all the levers. And there are a good number of people who struggle with managing spending on a monthly and weekly basis. Spending less is akin to going on a diet: it's no fun and no one wants to do it. But in the long run, living within your means today — whether in retirement or still working — could mean spending more down the road. Sometimes delaying gratification can lead to an increased level of happiness now and in the future.

Chapter 3
The Third Lever – Retirement Savings

Shell and Sid save their money

Meet Shell and Sid, who consider themselves to be part of Generation X. Shell found a love of computers in the 1980s when personal computing was just getting started. Shell always worked in technology and now runs the software development team of a technology company. Sid works as a registered nurse at a large hospital. Shell and Sid live outside of Charlotte, NC and both turn 55 this year. They have no money saved for retirement and that's OK!

Shell and Sid are both strong income earners. Working in tech has its perks, and one of them is a high salary. Shell's current role pays $175,000 per year with the opportunity to earn a bonus of $50,000, which pays out almost every year. So that puts Shell at $225,000. Sid works a lot of hours as a nurse. With the overtime, Sid typically earns about $90,000 per year. So that's $315,000 between the two of them, and they spend every penny!

Shell and Sid have a daughter, Kaley, who is finishing her last year at Duke. They sure are proud of Kaley but will not miss paying tuition. Kaley was able to get a small scholarship, student loans, and some help from her grandparents – every dollar counts! When it was all said and done, Shell and Sid ended up paying about $35,000 per year. They could swing it, but it hurt. In addition to funding the 4-year ~~party~~ educational experience, they live a big life. They have a nice house outside Charlotte, drive nice cars, and enjoy eating at nice restaurants. They spend all their income and even run up a few thousand dollars on a credit card from time to time.

After their neighbor told them about her financial planner, Shell and Sid decided to schedule a visit and see exactly how dire the situation was. Well, since they haven't saved anything, they weren't surprised to learn they need to make some changes. Neither of them has given any thought to when they might retire, or what they might do. The thought never crossed their mind. They are only 55 — retirement is for old people!

Since they haven't given much thought to retirement, they don't feel too strongly about when they wanted to retire. So, the retirement age lever is not really relevant. They enjoy their work and do not have any plans or desires to stop working. They always planned on working into their 70s. Even though nursing is hard work, Sid is already working on a transition to an administrative role that will be less physically demanding. And since they haven't made any firm plans for retirement, it's too soon to figure out how much they can spend in retirement. The most obvious lever to pull is increasing retirement savings. Like many people, they have no savings. Which is OK, but it needs to be addressed! And the best time to address it is today. Saving for retirement isn't too different from planting a tree... or at least not too different from this *proverb* about planting a tree. It goes like this: The best time to plant a tree (and start saving for retirement) is 10 years ago. The second best time to plant a tree (and start saving for retirement) is today!

Sometimes it is helpful to figure out, "How much do I need to save?" In the case of Shell and Sid, that question isn't relevant at this point and time. It's more important for them to ask, "How much can I save?" and then they should save as much as possible! That starts with a dreaded budget. How much money are they spending each month and where are they spending it? The first opportunity that will present itself to Sid and Shell is diverting the college tuition payments to retirement savings. They are already used to paying about $3,000 per month for tuition, so simply start saving $3,000 per month for retirement immediately after the payments end. Beyond that, they need to understand where they are spending their money. If they find themselves eating out two or three times per week, perhaps they could cut that back. Instead of renewing the lease on a top-of-the-line SUV with all the options, they could buy something used. There are a lot of options here.

Regardless of where they decide to spend their money, given they are 55 with no retirement savings, they should aim to save between 10 and 20% of their salary. That would be up to $63,000 per year. They have already identified $35,000 after diverting the tuition payments which puts them over 10%. That leaves another $28,000 if they want to get to 20%. Should they decide to retire at age 70, and they are able to save $35,000 per year with a 6% return on average, they might end up with over $800,000. That's quite a nest egg for retirement after starting with $0 at 55.

Pulling the retirement savings lever

Finally, we've arrived at a lever that might feel good. Retire later? That doesn't sound like much fun. Spend less in retirement? Terrible! But the practice of saving more, when executed properly and early enough, can change the trajectory of your retirement, and might even feel good while doing it.

This section will cover the various ways to increase your savings. Depending on your situation, the solution to saving more might be "keep doing what you are doing, just a little more" or, if all of these concepts are new to you, saving more might mean "begin to do this, that, and the other thing." Regardless of where you are on this spectrum, it's OK!

Now is a good time to review a couple of concepts before we get into the mechanics of saving more. First, we want to remind ourselves of the reason why we need to save more. We have done some kind of analysis, whether it is a full-blown financial plan with a financial professional or an online tool. And the result of that analysis was, let's just say, in need of improvement. So, you are not on track to spend what you want to spend in retirement. That's OK! The second thing we want to remind ourselves of is the concept of leverage. The more *time* we have until retirement, the more leverage we have with our savings.

And how did we arrive at the conclusion that we need to save more? Think back to our example calculations. The analysis has told us you are not on track. So now let's discuss that third lever: saving more. Your reaction might be, "Save more? I'm not saving anything! That's not part of my budget!" That's OK!

Why even save at all? About 50% of Americans don't have any retirement savings.[9] This situation needs improvement. Regardless of your situation, everyone working should be saving for retirement. Here are three significant benefits to saving for retirement.

First, by taking part of each paycheck and saving it for retirement, you are guaranteeing that you will always live beneath your means. The concept of living beneath your means can sound "preachy"; however, it's important to note that many financial difficulties begin with spending more than you earn. For example, if you earn $3,000 per month after taxes and save $300 per month, that leaves $2,700 to spend. Spending $2,700 while you earn $3,000 after taxes is living beneath your means. Saving part of your paycheck into a retirement account where it is very difficult to access the funds will help you achieve this. The $300 directed into a 401(k) or IRA cannot be spent. The other part of achieving this is not running up a bunch of credit card debt! Only spend what is earned and don't spend any more.

Second, by saving for retirement today, you will take advantage of the Power of Compound Interest. If you think back to the discussion about leverage, this is where the leverage becomes very important. The money you save today will grow. We will talk about how and why it grows later on. That money will grow over time. The more time you have before you need to use the money, the greater chance it will have to grow. And if the timeline is long enough, that growth may be significant.

Lastly, and this is almost a requirement if you want to maintain your current lifestyle throughout retirement, is the ability to grow an asset you can rely on in retirement, which will add to whatever guaranteed income sources you have.

The Social Security and private pension systems are a great benefit. And it is well outside the scope of this book to discuss if these programs are viable for the long-term, but let's generously assume they are. While they are a great benefit to millions of Americans, in many cases, people would like to have a lifestyle beyond their projected Social Security benefit. If you don't wish to have this lifestyle, then great! You probably don't need to save much money, and you can live off your Social Security when the time comes. But if you do wish to spend a little more in retirement, then that money needs to come from somewhere!

How do I save?

We are going to look at savings through two different lenses. The first lens is *how do I contribute to my retirement account?* There are two primary methods of saving for retirement. People can save through their employers, or they can save as individuals. The second lens is *what is the tax treatment of my retirement account?*

The most popular way to save for retirement is through an employer-sponsored plan. The mechanics of saving this way are quite simple. First, you have to work at a place that offers an employer-sponsored retirement plan. These plans come in lots of shapes and sizes. The most common plans are the 401(k), also known as a Profit Sharing Plan, a 403(b), a 457, and a SIMPLE IRA. If you work at a company, as opposed to being self-employed or working for a sole proprietor, your employer probably offers this to all its employees. In fact, 67% of companies offer some type of retirement plan according to the Bureau of Labor and Statistics.[10]

Once you have established that your company offers a retirement plan, the next step is to ENROLL in this plan.

Your manager, human resources manager, or the owner of the company can help you enroll. From here, you will need to elect how much of your salary to contribute and where you would like your money to be invested. Experts might agree on saving 10% to 15% of gross salary as a starting point. To make things even easier, legislative changes in the 2020s will require employers to automatically enroll employees in the company-sponsored plan.

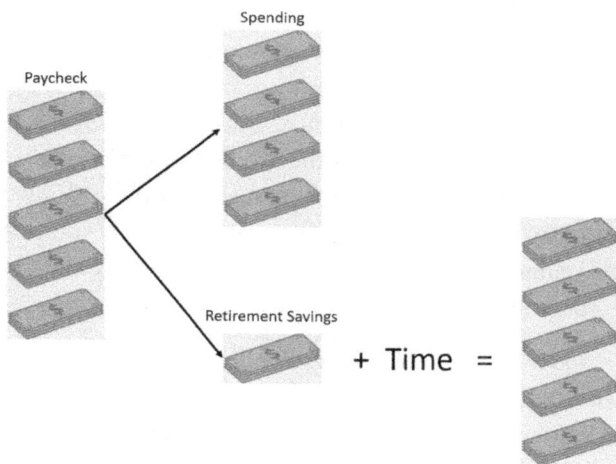

Note: the use of dollars is for illustrative purposes only. No one is guaranteed to achieve an increase in retirement savings solely due to time.

There's not a lot more to it than that. Here we've seen a couple of benefits of the employer-sponsored retirement savings plan. It's easy to get started. Once you start saving, the money will come directly out of your paycheck. It'll be like you never made the money. Determining how to invest the money may require some assistance — more on that later. But the odds are pretty good that the funds on the menu of options were selected by a group of investment professionals. After you've done the little bit of work to get started, the next step is the easy part: forget about it for 12 to 24 months. There's nothing else to do! Just watch your savings grow, check in on it every year or so, and go about living your life.

If your employer does not offer a retirement savings account, or maybe it does and you still wish to save even more, there are options for individual accounts. You may have heard of an Individual Retirement Account, also known as an IRA, or a Roth IRA. These are the two main types of individual accounts used for retirement.

The process to get started is roughly the same as if you were setting up a plan with your employer; however, there are a lot more options and less assistance. Rather than approaching your *one* employer to enroll in the *one retirement plan*, you must find a retirement account provider out of *hundreds*. While the options may be overwhelming, it is not difficult. If you simply search online for setting up an IRA, you will come across some good options.

Once you decide on where you will open your IRA, also known as your *custodian*, you will have to decide which type of investments to invest in. This is the same idea as the custodian of someone's kids should they pass away: who is taking care of your funds. Here is where things can get a little more complicated. As opposed to the 401(k), which probably has a menu of 10-20 investment options, your IRA provider probably has 1,000 different investments on the platform. We will go into more detail later.

After you have decided how to invest your money, it's time to fund the account. Instead of saving the money from your paycheck, you will have to move the money from your bank account. You could do this as a one-time transaction. Ideally, you will set up a monthly recurring transaction to automatically save the same amount at the same time every month. This will have the same benefit as saving from your paycheck. As long as it happens automatically, it will be like you never had the money in the first place. Like your employer retirement plan, once you set it up, you can forget about it for 12-24 months, let the savings accumulate, then check in on it down the road. Think of this as your "retirement subscription." The same way people set up an automatic payment for Netflix, Verizon, and the like, the best way to save is to set up an auto pay to yourself.

The second lens to look through is *what is the tax treatment of my retirement account?* In order to understand the tax treatment of our accounts, we are going to use a concept called The Tax Control Triangle[11]. Sorry for the geometry but luckily, triangles aren't too advanced!

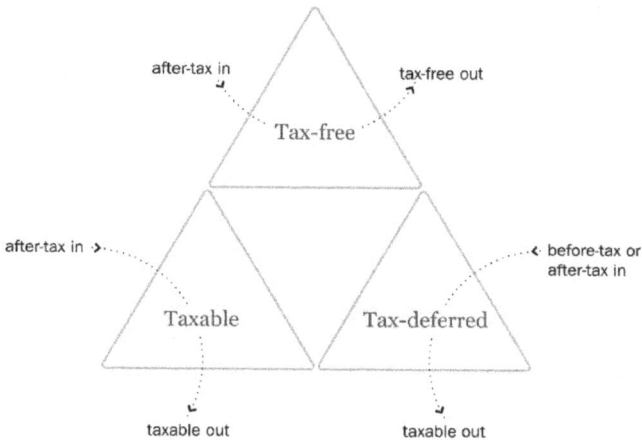

The first leg of the triangle, in the bottom right corner, is what's called Tax Deferred. This means we are going to contribute to our account now and defer our taxes to a later date. The classic examples of Tax Deferred accounts are:

- 401(k), also known as Profit Sharing
- 403(b), like a 401(k) for non-profit organizations
- 457, a deferred compensation plan for government employees
- TSP, Thrift Savings Plan for federal employees
- IRA, a Traditional Individual Retirement Account
- SIMPLE IRA, like a 401(k) for companies with under 100 employees

These account types all have various rules and details around how they work. But they are all treated the same for tax purposes; that is, they are all Tax Deferred.

What exactly makes something Tax Deferred? For that, we need an example. Let's say you work at a job with a 401(k), and you earn $50,000 per year. You decide to contribute 10% of your salary, or $5,000 per year to your 401(k). If you are paid bi-weekly, that would be $192 per paycheck. That $192 per paycheck will be directed to your 401(k). It's as if you never made the money. So, you'll get $192 less in your paycheck, and over the course of 12 months, from January 1st to December 31st, you will save a total of $5,000 to your 401(k). Now when you go to file your taxes, it will be like you never made the $5,000. If your gross salary is $50,000, your W2 gross wages will only be $45,000 and therefore, you have not yet paid taxes on your contributions. This is the first form of tax deferral.

The Four Levers

Gross Paycheck   Retirement Savings   Taxable Income

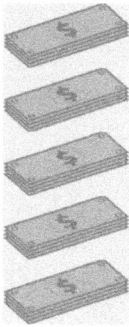

What happens next? Now comes the exciting part, hopefully you will watch your investment grow over time. That $5,000 will be invested in something, hopefully some appropriate mix of stocks and bonds, which we will discuss later, and then we have to do the really boring part: wait until retirement. Maybe you are 10, 20, or even 40 years out from retirement. Here's where the second form of tax deferral comes in. The tax on the investment gain — and let's hope over 20 or 30 years there is a sizeable gain on your investment — is deferred. The second form of tax deferral is not paying any taxes on those gains until 20 or 30 years later when you withdraw the money.

Now, you fast forward to retirement. Let's say your $5,000 grew by 6% over 20 years. It's now worth roughly $15,000. OK, it's $16,035 if you want to use the time value of money formula. You have not yet paid any taxes on the $5,000 you originally earned but saved to your 401(k), nor have you paid any taxes on the gain of $11,035. This is the Tax Deferral. Now, when you withdraw your money in retirement, you will pay taxes on whatever you withdraw. This a great opportunity to save and grow money with no tax implications until retirement.

Retirement Savings

Future Retirement Savings

 + Time =

Not taxed here   Finally taxed here

Note: the use of dollars is for illustrative purposes only. No one is guaranteed to achieve an increase in retirement savings solely due to time.

The second leg of the triangle is arguably the best leg of the triangle. It's commonly called the Tax-Free leg, or the Roth leg. The most common types of Tax-Free accounts are:

- Roth IRA
- Roth 401(k)
- Roth 403(b)
- Some people might put a 529 plan and a Health Savings Account in this leg.

Again, these accounts have different rules and features, but they are all treated the same for tax purposes, that is, they are Tax-Free. That is not a typo, they are free from any income tax. It may seem too good to be true, but it really is true!

Let's talk about what makes them "Tax-Free." The first major difference from the Tax Deferred accounts is we will pay taxes on the money contributed. This is what's commonly called "after-tax" contributions. To use the same example as before, you work at a job but instead of a 401(k), you will contribute to a Roth 401(k). You earn $50,000 per year and you decide to contribute $5,000 per year to the Roth 401(k). The math is the same, you will save $192 per paycheck and a total of $5,000 over the course of 12 months. Here is the first major difference: your gross salary is $50,000 and you will not get a deduction for your contribution. Your contributions are essentially taxed, meaning your contributions are after-tax.

That's the first major difference; the second major difference is where the magic happens. So same as above, you fast forward to retirement. Let's say your $5,000 grew by the same 6% over 20 years and it's now worth roughly the same $15,000. To recap, you contributed $5,000 which you paid taxes on, and now you have a $10,000 gain on your investment. Are you ready for the best part: you will pay NO taxes on the $10,000 gain when you withdraw your funds. This seems too good to be true, but it's not! Roth, aka Tax Free, accounts are a very important tool in managing your retirement investments.

And now we've arrived at the final leg, the taxable leg. What makes this leg special is that it is not special at all. There is no special tax treatment for any taxable account. You may see these classic taxable accounts:

- Any joint account: CDs, Brokerage
- Any account held in a trust
- Any individual account that is not in a Tax Deferred or Tax Free

People call these accounts Non-Qualified, meaning they are not "qualified" for any special tax treatment. In other words, they're not *magical.*

Let's use the same example to describe the major differences with these accounts. Instead of a Roth 401(k) or a 401(k), you have decided to contribute to a joint brokerage account with your spouse. You earn the same $50,000 and you will save $5,000 over the course of the year. So, if these accounts get no special tax treatment, do you think you are allowed to deduct the $5,000 contribution from your salary? No! So, you will pay taxes on the $5,000 contribution, making your contributions "after-tax." Then if you use the same investment, your $5,000 will grow to $15,000 over the course of 20 years meaning you had an investment gain of $10,000. If you get no special tax treatment on this account, do you think you pay taxes on the $10,000 gain? Yes!

When you pay the taxes and at what rate you pay the taxes gets a little complicated, but if you hold the investment for a long time, more than a year, you will pay a more favorable long-term capital gains tax rate. If you hold the investment for a short time, less than a year, you will pay the less favorable income tax rates. The taxes for the long-term gains are calculated separately at a typically lower rate than your income tax. The taxes for the short-term gains are added to your taxable income and taxed at your income tax rate. And if your investment pays you income, for example interest from a bank account or dividends from a stock, you will actually pay those taxes each year over the 20 years.

If these accounts get no special tax treatment, why use them for retirement at all? That's a complicated question but here are a few common reasons when this may be beneficial for retirement:

The Four Levers

- Tax-deferred and Tax-free accounts have contribution limits and income limitations. If you wish to save more than these limits, or are above the income limitations, you would have to use a taxable accounts to save for retirement.
- Even without special tax treatment, having some assets in this "bucket" can help diversify your tax base in retirement.
- If you have significant assets you have held for a long time, the capital gains tax rates you will pay on a taxable account may be more favorable than the income tax rates you will pay on a tax-deferred account. This does not apply to Roth accounts — nothing beats paying no taxes! This would also be true for assets you hold for a long time and leave to heirs. The heirs would pay very little taxes compared to what you would have paid; they might even pay no taxes depending on the final disposition of the assets.
- You may be able to take advantage of the lowest long-term capital gains tax rate, which is currently 0%, and is better than any ordinary income tax rate you would pay on IRA distributions. This situation is quite rare, but it is possible.
- You may want to retire before 59 ½ and this is the easiest way to access retirement money before this age.

In addition to each leg of the triangle having benefits independently, it is also a strong strategy to balance how much investments you have in each leg of the triangle. Recall when each leg of the triangle is taxed:

- Tax-Deferred – taxed in retirement as income tax.
- Tax-Free – never taxed!

- Taxable – taxed either each year or as a more favorable long-term capital gain.

Why is this important? In retirement, there are several factors that will determine your taxable income and it will be the highest priority to *minimize* your income. The first reason is, due to the progressive nature of our income tax system, the higher your income, the higher your tax rate. Meaning if you have a high income, the tax you pay on your 401(k) or IRA withdrawals will be higher relative to someone with a lower income. The second reason is, as your income increases, other taxes kick in such as making taxable your Social Security and additional premiums for Medicare. Medicare is still a great deal, even with the surcharges, but no one wants to pay the surcharges!

Balancing the legs of the triangle can be a challenge, and the later you begin balancing the legs, the harder it is to do. There are several compelling reasons to put money into each of the buckets. And the interaction between those compelling reasons makes the financial planning process as much of an art as a science. Understanding the benefits of a unique savings strategy for *your* situation may require the help of a professional. This is where financial planning software earns its money.

The Four Levers

Putting financial planning software aside, here are a few broad strategies and considerations for maximizing the use of the triangle:

- Most people assume, usually correctly, that they will be in a lower tax bracket in retirement, relative to their tax bracket in their peak earning years. If this is the case, it's probably best to contribute to a Tax Deferred account, such as the 401(k) or IRA. The strategy here is you will defer taxes on your contributions while in a higher bracket, then withdraw the money in retirement when you are in a relatively lower bracket. Projecting tax brackets, not only what the tax brackets will be, but also what tax bracket you will be in, 10, 20, or 40 years into the future is a challenging task to put it mildly, but this is generally true for a lot of people.
- Maximize contributions to a Roth or Tax-Free account. This is a top priority for tax diversification. The tax-free growth makes this very appealing for practically everyone. The only downsides to the Roth are two limitations. First, the annual contribution limit to a Roth IRA is lower relative to a 401(k), meaning you can accumulate more assets in a 401(k) than a Roth IRA, based on contribution limits. And second, there are income limitations, meaning if you earn above a certain amount in any given year, you are not allowed to contribute to a Roth IRA. Not to be confused with the Roth 401(k) when it is available. The Roth 401(k) has the same contribution limits as the 401(k). The main point here is to take advantage of Tax-Free accounts that are available to you.
- If you think your income will vary drastically in the years leading up to retirement, early retirement, or

63

deep into retirement, two things become very important. First, you will want to have money in each side of the triangle to draw on. Having a diversified tax base in retirement will allow you to have more control over your income. For example, the Roth funds are tax-free which has two benefits: you will not pay taxes on any of the gains, and those withdrawals will not affect your taxable income for the year. So, in a retirement year where your income is higher for whatever reason, you can use funds from a Roth account to not increase your retirement income any further. And conversely, in a year where your income is lower, you can draw from Tax-Deferred accounts to take advantage of potentially lower tax rates. Second, if your income is highly variable, you may be able to take advantage of strategies to actually *move* money from one side of the triangle to another, thus furthering your diversification without major tax impacts.

Regardless of how your retirement account is treated for tax purposes, one thing you will almost certainly want to take advantage of is your employer's matching contribution. Many people will call this the "company match." I call it "free money." This discussion only applies to a retirement plan you have access to through your employer, such as a 401(k), SIMPLE IRA, or 403(b). This does not apply to any individual retirement plan such as an Individual Retirement Account (IRA) or Roth IRA.

Since 401(k) plans account for the majority of retirement accounts, let's discuss how the 401(k) works in detail. There are four ways to contribute funds into your 401(k).

The Four Levers

- Pre-tax contributions through payroll deduction. Remember what makes the 401(k) pre-tax – you will make contributions and those contributions will be deducted from your income in the year you make the contribution. This happens through a payroll deduction. You will fill out a form instructing your employer on how much you wish to contribute to your 401(k). Some people choose a percentage of their salary and others choose a flat dollar amount. Regardless of how much you choose, it will be deducted from your pay automatically and sent to your 401(k) account.

- Roth 401(k) contributions through payroll deduction. This works exactly as the pre-tax contributions; however, the amount you contribute will not be deducted from your taxable income. This is what makes these contributions "after-tax." Remember that these contributions will grow completely tax-free. Your employer has to offer the Roth 401(k) as an option in the retirement plan in order to make these types of contributions.

- After-tax contributions through payroll deduction. This is a slightly nuanced option and the employer has to offer this as an option in the retirement plan. Many people confuse this option with the Roth option. They are similar in that the contributions are not deducted for tax purposes, thus making them after-tax contributions. The main difference is the money does not grow tax-free, you will pay taxes on the earnings, unlike the Roth, where you pay no taxes on the earnings. Why would anyone choose this option? The main advantage to the after-tax contributions is you can contribute above and beyond the standard contribution limits to your pre-tax and Roth options. This is subject to your employer offering this option; not all employer-sponsored plans offer it.

- Employer matching contributions. Many employers will choose to contribute to the employee's retirement plan. This is a very standard offering as part of any compensation package. The employer makes contributions to the employee retirement plan as a benefit to the employee, while also encouraging the employee to save for retirement by "matching" what the employee contributes. A common formula for determining how much the employer will contribute is to match the employee contributions up to a certain percentage. A typical matching program might look like: The employer matches 100% of the employee contributions up to 3% of the employee's salary. For example, the employee earns $50,000 per year and decides to contribute $77 per bi-weekly paycheck. This amounts to about $2,000 per year, or 4% of the employee's salary. In this example, the employer would match those contributions up to a maximum of $1,500, or 3% of $50,000. That's a nice little bonus!

- Employer discretionary contributions. While the employer matching contributions is a very common benefit, a much less common benefit is an employer making a contribution solely at the discretion of the owner or company leadership. The employer can make this decision on the basis of many factors and this is typically treated as a "bonus" or "profit sharing." While it can be great to contribute to employee retirement accounts, if the contributions are not consistent, it can be difficult for the

employee to count on these contributions for
retirement planning.

An important consideration in determining how much to
contribute to your retirement plan is to learn about the
company's contribution matching benefit. You almost
certainly want to contribute to the retirement plan to receive
the full matching amount. If you contribute less than the full
matching amount, or nothing at all, you are leaving money on
the table. Your employer is providing a financial benefit you
are not taking advantage of. Many people call this "free
money." And they are correct!

Mike Kendra

Pre-tax savings opportunities (note: all contribution limits are as of 2023)

Account Type	Description	Employer or Individual	Annual Contribution Limits	How to start
401(k)	Classic retirement plan offered through employer	Employer	$22,500 per year plus $7,500 if you are 50 or older	Contribute through payroll deduction and may be eligible for employer matching contributions.
403(b)	Similar to 401(k) for non-profits and local government employees	Employer	$22,500 per year plus $7,500 if you are 50 or older	Contribute through payroll deduction.
457 Plan	Non-qualified deferred compensation plan for government employees	Employer	$22,500 per year plus $7,500 if you are 50 or older	Contribute through payroll deduction.
Thrift Savings Plan	Similar to 401(k) for Federal Employees	Employer	$22,500 per year plus $7,500 if you are 50 or older	Contribute through payroll deduction. Limited fund selection
SIMPLE IRA	Similar to 401(k) for a small business	Employer	$15,500 per year plus $3,500 if you are 50 or older	Contribute through payroll deduction. Eligible for

	(100 employees or less)			employer matching contributions.
Traditional IRA	Individual Retirement Account	Individual	$6,500 per year plus $1,000 if you are 50 or older	Offered through any of the hundreds of brokerage firms.

Tax-Free savings opportunities

Account Type	Description	Employer or Individual	Contribution limits	Notes
Roth 401(k), 403(b), 457	Roth plans established as part of a 401(k), 403(b), or 457	Employer	Same as pre-tax for 401(k), 403(b), and 457. Total pre-tax and Roth contributions cannot exceed the limit.	Retirement plan must establish this option.
Roth IRA	Individual Retirement Account	Individual	Same as Traditional IRA. Total Traditional and Roth IRA contributions cannot exceed the limit.	Offered through any of the hundreds of brokerage firms.
Health Savings Account	Plan offered to cover qualified medical expenses	Can be offered through employer or individual	$3,850 for an individual or $7,700 if married filing jointly plus $1,000 if you are 50 or older	Distributions must be used for qualified medical expenses. Contributions are also tax-deferred.

Chapter 4
The Fourth Lever – Take An Appropriate Amount of Risk

Matt and Madison manage their risk

Matt served as a police officer for 30 years. Matt decided he wanted to become an officer of the law as a child and joined the Oregon State Police right out of college. After serving 30 years, Matt took on a second career as a grief counselor. Matt and Madison married young, raised three kids, and recently emptied out the nest. Madison works as a school librarian. Matt and Madison don't like to take a lot of risk; they like "sure things" such as the Oregon pension system, cash, and the ordered logic of a library.

Liking "sure things" has its benefits. Matt and Madison are each eligible for a pension at retirement. They also like to put aside money "just in case." Neither of them enjoyed spending money. They would rather spend their time hiking, reading, or visiting with their children. This results in some extra money each month. They never really figured out what to do with the money, so they just let it sit in a savings account at the bank.

As the years went by, Matt and Madison's salaries increased, slowly and steadily. The increases amounted to a couple percentage points each year which was again, a sure thing for government employees. And while the salaries went up, their spending never really went up with it. So, they just automatically saved the money. Over the past 25 years, they had about $1,000 left over each month leaving them with almost $400,000 in cash at the bank.

Having $400,000 in the bank is a great thing; however, here is one of the downsides to liking a "sure thing". In the investment world, the "sure thing" does not have much potential to grow. Over 25 years, the savings account at the bank has barely paid 2% interest on average. While it is better than nothing, there are other investments which could experience a higher return if they are willing to take more risk. By nature, Matt and Madison do not have a high tolerance for risk. This is a personal decision, but they should also consider the nature of their full retirement picture. And the nature of their full retirement picture is a "sure thing." That is, it's guaranteed. It's practically risk-free. They each have a pension from their years of service as a police officer and educator. They also have Social Security. Their entire retirement is risk-free. Therefore, considering the full extent of their retirement assets, perhaps they could consider taking some risk with the money they have saved, since it wouldn't be as risky for them as it would be for others who do not have the "sure-thing" retirement picture they do.

They are only in their mid-50s and are thinking of working for 10 more years. So, it may be appropriate, after consulting with a professional, to consider pulling the risk lever and investing in a balanced portfolio of stocks and bonds with their money. By no means should they take all the $400,000 and invest in a few risky stocks. That would be too much risk for Matt and Madison. But after carving out a comfortable amount to keep in cash, say $50,000, they might consider investing $350,000, putting $175,000 in a mix of bonds and $175,000 in a mix of high-quality stocks. While there is the potential to lose money in the short term, over the next 10 or 15 years, the balanced portfolio of stocks and bonds will most likely significantly outperform a savings account at the bank.

Pulling the risk lever

After exploring several different ways to save and the tax implications of using various savings vehicles, it's important to understand how to actually invest your money. But before understanding stocks and bonds, which is the primary way to invest your money, it's important to understand "risk." What is risk and how does it present itself in the context of investments? This is our fourth lever.

Risk can be defined in different ways, depending on the context. A broad definition of risk is "variation in expected outcome." Let's take something simple like the weather. It's July in the southern part of the United States, let's say Florida. What is the possible variation in the daily high temperature in Florida in July? On a mild day, it might be in the mid-80s, and on a warm day, it might be in the upper 90s or even 100. One way to express the risk of the high temperature would be to establish an average, or expected value and a likely range. Using our example, the expected high temperature is probably 93 degrees, and the possible range is about 10 degrees. In practical terms, almost all the time, the high temperature will be between 83 and 103 degrees.

Applying this concept to investments, we need to understand the concept of investment return. What exactly is investment return? It is an increase (or decrease) in the value of our investment. Determining the expected return on our investment will help us plan for our retirement. And how do we determine the expected return? We will turn to history, while keeping in mind that historical returns may or may not be repeated in the future. It is not perfect, and it is in no way guaranteed, but it is a useful starting point for understanding what we can expect our investments to return. Because this is an important component of your retirement planning, investment performance needs to be continually monitored. In the case where your investments do not perform up to historical averages, you may have to make adjustments to your retirement plan. This is what makes retirement planning a *process*.

After understanding the concept of risk — that is, the variation in expected return of our investments — we next need to answer the question: how much risk do I need to take? To answer how much risk to take, we must consider three main factors: personal risk tolerance, time horizon, and personal objectives.

Your personal risk tolerance can be summed up in the question, "How well will you sleep at night knowing you are invested a certain way?" How much risk a person is willing to take is largely innate. The spectrum of risk-taking can go from "I want to keep all of my money underneath my mattress" on one end to "I am only happy running eight different businesses exposing all of my personal wealth to the success of each business." People will naturally fall somewhere on the spectrum at a place that may or may not be appropriate for their situation. With some coaching and advice, people can easily arrive at an investment strategy where they are taking an appropriate amount of risk for their situation. Generally speaking, the higher our personal risk tolerance, the more investment risk we can feel comfortable taking.

Your time horizon is simply answering the question: "When will I need the money?" This is directly tied to your goal and understanding when you plan on achieving your goal. If wish to retire at age 65, your time horizon is 20 years when you are 45, 10 years when you are 55, and so on. And keep in mind the nuance of retirement length. Expanding the example, if you wish to retire at 65 and you are now 55, your time horizon is 10 years until the *start* of retirement. If your life expectancy is 85, you will need *some* of your money in 10 years, but you also won't need some of your money for 15 years, 20 years, or 30 years. This can be a complicated idea because "retirement" is not a single event, it could possibly be a 30-year or 40-year phase of life. So, it's important to consider that people's time horizon for retirement is not one number, it is a series of numbers and we have to consider this for our time horizon. This is where financial planning software comes in handy! Generally speaking, the longer our time horizon, the more investment risk we can feel comfortable taking.

Your personal objective is simply answering the question, "What will I do with the money?" Again, this is directly tied to the goal and inextricably linked from the time horizon. On one end of the spectrum, your goal may be to simply maintain the value of your investment. If your goal is to make a down payment on a home or pay for your child's education in a few years, you are probably not willing to see the value of your investment decrease; you simply wish to maintain its value. On the other end of the spectrum, if you have a goal to retire in the future with an increased lifestyle, your objective is more oriented to growing your assets to not only outpace inflation, but also allow for an increased lifestyle. Here, you may be willing to take more risk for the potential of investment growth. Generally speaking, if our objective is to grow our investment, we need to be comfortable taking more risk.

To summarize:

- Higher personal risk tolerance higher investment risk
- Lower personal risk tolerance lower investment risk
- Longer time horizon higher investment risk
- Shorter time horizon lower investment risk
- Personal objective is growth higher investment risk
- Personal objective is preserving investment value lower investment risk

The next step after answering these questions is to put investors into a category known as Investment Risk Profile. Here, we are going to put people on another spectrum. On one end of the spectrum is a conservative investor and on the other end of the spectrum is an aggressive investor. And in between, there are some well-established blends.

Conservative	Moderate Conservative	Moderate	Moderate Aggressive	Aggressive

The previous few paragraphs describe more of the "science" of risk profile, but in reality, it is also an "art." What one person describes as Moderate, another person may describe as Moderate Aggressive, and vice versa. Here is another topic where an investment professional can help tremendously. Figuring this out on your own can be a challenge, and a true professional will guide you in the right direction.

The Four Levers

What are we actually going to do with this information? We are going to develop something called an investment or asset allocation. This is where we decide exactly how to invest our money. Here there are four main options, or asset classes:

- Stocks, or equities
- Bonds, or fixed income
- Cash
- Alternative investments such as real estate, commodities, precious metals and the like

For the purposes of our asset allocation discussion, we are going to exclude cash and alternatives, primarily to keep things simple while also avoiding the very deep rabbit hole of alternative investments. Additionally, the allocation to cash and alternatives is typically a small percentage of an overall allocation, perhaps 2-5%, so disregarding these two asset classes for our discussion will not have a material impact. And tying back to a safe withdrawal rate, keeping 2-5% in cash makes sense for someone who is going to withdraw that amount each year. (Note: it is my belief that this entire book is largely free of controversy, but this may be the most controversial point. The horror!)

Before we arrive at how to invest our money, it's helpful to have a working definition of these asset classes. Stocks, or equities, are ownership slices of a company. Most people are familiar with large corporations such as Apple, Verizon, General Electric, Boeing, Exxon Mobile, General Motors, and Amazon. These are all publicly traded companies. Anyone, with practically any amount of money, can go into the market and purchase shares of these companies. People (investors, shareholders) are buying and selling shares of these companies every day, all day long. And as a "nonprofessional," it's as easy as a few clicks on your computer or smart phone. In many respects, it's *too easy*, to the point of getting into trouble unintentionally.

Why does anyone buy shares of a company? There are two main reasons. First, the investor believes that the value of the company will increase over time. They believe the company will grow their business through increasing their existing sales, adding product lines, creating new services, and the like. When a company grows over time, the value of a share of that company typically increases. Thus, an investor can buy a share at one point in time at one price, then sell it many years later at what is hopefully a higher price. This is the famed "buy low and sell high." The second reason is to collect a piece of the company's earnings. While it can be difficult for a company to earn a profit at the beginning of their life as a company, over time they eventually *must* earn a profit; otherwise, they will go out of business. When a company starts to earn profits, they have two choices around what to do with the profits. They can either reinvest the profits back into the company in the form of buying equipment, investing in people, creating new product lines, etc. Or they can distribute the profits to the owners, in this case the shareholders. This comes in the form of a dividend. Practically speaking, most companies do a combination of both. They take some of their profits and reinvest it into the company. Then, they pay a dividend to the shareholders. As the investor, this is best case scenario. The investor is generating income simply by owning the share of the company. The investor gets to decide what to do with the dividend. One option is to take the dividend as cash. Like any cash payment, it's incredibly flexible because you can use it for anything. The other option is to take your dividend payment and purchase more shares of the company.

This is where the idea of compound growth starts to pay off. Your original investment starts to pay dividends, then when you reinvest the dividends, those shares start to pay dividends.

The second major asset class is bonds, or fixed income. Instead of owning a slice of a company in the case of a stock, a bond investor is acting like a bank. The investor is loaning money to the company. Why would anyone loan money to a company? The same reason the bank loans people money for a house or a car: they wish to receive the interest payments. To keep things simple for our discussion, we are going to limit the scope of bonds to US Treasuries. There are three main bond markets:

- The US Government borrows money to fund ongoing federal spending – these are US Treasuries.
- US Corporations borrow money to fund various projects and investments – these are US Corporate Bonds.
- State and Local governments borrow money to fund projects and occasionally ongoing spending – these are Municipal Bonds.

For our discussion, we are going to consider only the interest earned on the money loaned (remember: the investor is the bank loaning money to the government or corporations.) There are several considerations when investing in bonds which will be outside the scope of our discussion. This is a partial list, just to give you an idea if you'd like to explore further yourself:

- Bonds are issued and then traded on a market similar to stocks. We are going to disregard any impact the secondary market has on the price of our bond investment.

- Changing interest rates will impact the price of our bond investment.
- Who we loan our money to will also impact our investment. If there is an increased risk that they will not pay back the loan, that will impact the price of our bond investment.

These concepts can get complicated very quickly, so for the purpose of our discussion, we are going to consider only US Treasuries. And we will further assume that we hold them to maturity. In other words, we invest our money into a US Treasury Bond, collect our interest every six months, then at the end of the term, we collect our original investment. Making these assumptions allows us to disregard the considerations described above. If we hold our bonds to maturity, any changes in interest rates will not impact our investment. And let's all agree that there is no risk of the United States federal government not paying people back! If the US federal government doesn't pay back bonds, we all have bigger problems!

These considerations are what make some people argue bonds are a "safer" investment than stocks. We can examine "safe" from two vantage points. The first vantage point is: what is the absolute most I can lose from my investment? Here's the bad news with stocks. Don't let this scare you because there are techniques to prevent this, but you can, in theory, lose all your money with stocks. In the worst-case scenario, you own shares of a company and when that company goes bankrupt, or completely out of business, there is a very good likelihood the value of your shares will decrease to $0. Meaning whatever you originally invested is worthless.

Whereas, specifically with US Treasuries, there is no chance you will lose any of your money as long as the United States is around. So, to summarize the first vantage point: with a stock, although very unlikely, you can theoretically lose all your money; with a bond, specifically a US Treasury, you cannot lose any money. Obviously from this perspective, this makes bonds a "safer" investment.

The second vantage point is: how much will the value of my investment vary over the years? This is known as *volatility*. With stocks — and again this shouldn't scare you — the value of your shares will increase and decrease significantly over the years. Remember back to how someone buys shares of a company – they go to the market to buy or sell. Every day, all day long, people are buying and selling shares. Over any given period of time, the price of those shares will vary based on a wide array of factors. Here is a partial list of those factors:

- Company increases or decreases sales significantly.
- Company launches new successful product.
- CEO is charged with criminal activity.
- Competitors go out of business.
- War, terrorism, or political unrest strikes.
- Change to overall economic conditions occurs.

Information about these companies becomes "news" and this "news" affects the price of the shares. Little news, little change in the price of the shares. Big news, big change in the price of the shares. How much can the price change? In any given year, the shares of any given company may increase or decrease by 30, 40, even 60%. Seeing the value of your investment decrease by 60% does not sound very appealing, but again, this is both unlikely and somewhat simple to mitigate. Here's the other good news with bonds: as long as we limit our discussion to US treasuries and hold these bonds to maturity, the value of our bonds will never increase or decrease. We are only going to collect interest payments and not worry about the factors mentioned above such as changes in interest rates or the creditworthiness of the borrower. At maturity, the investment principal is returned, and therefore, none of these factors have a practical effect on our bonds if we are going to hold them to maturity.

So, bonds are the clear winner in the "safe" category. As long as you hold them to maturity, you cannot lose any of your money by investing in US Treasuries, nor will you experience any swings in the value of your investment. Given this conclusion, why would anyone invest in anything other than bonds?

The answer to that question is somewhat simple: higher risk means higher reward. If we want a higher reward than what we'd get from bonds, we need to take additional risk by owning stocks in order to potentially receive a higher return over the long term. And the reason we need to seek higher potential returns over the long-term is because of inflation. Inflation is a complicated topic, and if you ask five different professionals to explain inflation, you will probably get five different answers. For this discussion, let's concern ourselves only with the prices we experience as a consumer. And in these terms, inflation is the increase in the prices we experience. And again, for simplicity's sake, let's assume that this is generally *bad*. If today we buy groceries for a family of four and it costs on average $200, and then 3 years later the same shopping basket of groceries costs $210, you need to earn more money to buy the same level of goods. This is how people experience inflation. Over the past several decades, including periods where inflation spiked higher and dropped lower, inflation has averaged about 3% per year. Using our grocery example, we need to earn 3% more per year to be able to afford the same amount of groceries.

What does this have to do with investing? If you think back to our original retirement goal, we wish, at some point in the future, to stop working and continue to live relatively the same lifestyle. In order for this to successfully occur, we need to not only save money, but we will need that money to grow. And not only do we need that money to grow, but we also need that money to grow much, much more than the rate of inflation.

Historically speaking, our very safe bonds have returned 3-5%, depending on the maturity and the type of bond we owned. This is a good, but not great, return. And it may or may not outpace inflation. To readdress our question from a few paragraphs ago, why would anyone invest in anything other than bonds? Because we need the potential higher growth of stocks, which historically is in the 7% to 10% range, depending on the time frame and the type of stocks we have invested in. In the case where our past stocks earned 8.5% over a period of time, if inflation was about 3% over that same period of time, those investment significantly outpaced inflation.

If you're feeling somewhat skeptical, you might be asking, "Aren't stocks risky?" Yes, they are! And here is how we are going to mitigate some of that risk: *diversification*. Diversification is a very important concept, and we will address two kinds of diversification. First, we will diversify our investments by investing in both stocks and bonds. To use the example from *A Random Walk Down Wall Street* by Burton Malkiel, this is like a store selling sunscreen and umbrellas. On a sunny day, the sunscreen will sell and on rainy days, the umbrellas will sell. And the total sales over a long period of time will be better than if you sold only umbrellas or only sunscreen. And not only will the overall sales be higher, but you will also experience less variation along the way. If you sold only umbrellas or only sunscreen, there would be a lot of days where you experienced "$0" sales, whereas if you sold both umbrellas and sunscreen, you would have a lot *fewer* days with "$0" sales. This variation is called *volatility,* and the main benefit of diversification is you will experience less volatility.

The second way to diversify your investments is within the stocks and bonds in a portfolio. An investor's portfolio does not include only *one* stock and only *one* bond. A standard investment model portfolio includes hundreds, or possibly thousands of stocks and bonds. This is known as "not putting all your eggs in one basket." If we own exactly one stock, and that company happens to go out of business, that would be catastrophic to our portfolio! If one stock we own happens to go out of business, which is quite rare, it won't really affect our portfolio if we own 999 other stocks and 1,000 other bonds. While it would be terrible, we might not even notice a change in our portfolio.

Diversifying is a very important concept, and it's actually not that difficult to do. The first step in diversifying is to understand what mix of stocks and bonds is appropriate for your situation. Remember the considerations: time horizon, investment objectives, and personal risk tolerance. Investors are categorized on a spectrum from *Aggressive* to *Conservative*. Figuring out where you are on this spectrum can be a challenge and this would be an appropriate time to consult with a financial professional. Determining where you are on the spectrum involves answering several questions such as:

- What is your financial goal for these funds?

The Four Levers

- When do you expect to need these funds?
- How would you feel if your funds lost value?
- How much of a decrease in value can you stomach? 10%? 30%? 50%?
- Can you stomach a significant short-term loss in value in exchange for the possibility of a significant long-term increase in value?

Answering these questions will put you on a scale of zero to 100. To keep things simple, the number on the scale equates to the percentage of the portfolio invested in stocks. Here are two examples. These examples are for reference only and are not customized to any investor's situation.

For the first example:

- What is your financial goal for these funds? **Retirement.**
- When do you expect to need these funds? **30+ years.**
- How would you feel if you your funds lost value? **Feel OK if investments lose value. Would be OK if the investments lost 50% in value in the short-term with the hopes of doubling the money twice over 30 years.**

These answers would be more of a classic *Aggressive* investor, and they might be a 90 or even 100 on the scale. Meaning this person could invest 90% or even 100% in stocks.

For the second example, here are the answers to the questions above:

- What is your financial goal for these funds? **Retirement.**
- When do you expect to need these funds? **10 years.**
- How would you feel if your funds lost value? **Feel OK if investments lose value. Would be OK if the investments lost 20% in value in the short-term with the hopes of doubling the money once over 10 years.**

These answers would be more of a *Conservative* investor, and they might be a 50 or 60 on the scale. Meaning this person could invest 50% in stocks and 50% in bonds. The conservative investor will not likely experience a significant decrease in the value of their investment. This is the beauty of diversification.

This brief introduction to investments covered an overview of investing in stocks and bonds, while explaining how much of a portfolio might be invested in one or the other. And with this piece of understanding, the fourth and final lever appears: Take an appropriate amount of risk. This is a lever that must be used with a great level of care. When we compare this lever to the other three levers, this is the only lever that might cause harm. Think about the first three:

- Delay retirement. You might not like it, but there's no harm in delaying your retirement. You'll stay out of trouble longer while delaying pulling from your nest egg.
- Reduce spending. It might not be fun, but there's no harm in reducing your planned spending. No one

ever said, "Gee it's too bad I have $300 left over from last month."

- Increase savings. It may be hard to do, but it will never hurt to save more. People with $1,000,000 in a 401(k) never said, I wish I would have blown that money on something silly, rather than have a huge nest egg for retirement.

Contrast that with our fourth lever, taking risk, which can be more precisely explained as *taking the appropriate amount of risk*. Here are three simple ways to think about using this lever:

- Someone is already taking an appropriate amount of risk; don't pull the lever!
- Someone is approaching retirement and not sure what is an appropriate amount of risk; don't pull the lever!
- Someone has a long, long time until retirement and is not exposed to any stocks; seek assistance and possibly pull the lever with caution.

While this lever is very important, the use of the lever is highly customized. Before using the lever, each person needs to have a good understanding of their current risk tolerance, time horizon, personal objectives, and their current investment allocation. Then they can determine if this is appropriate. It would be negligent to put forward a "rule of thumb" or general guideline. People who are unsure how to navigate this section should seek the help of an investment professional.

To summarize the four levers, there are four levers that people can pull as the four main inputs to any retirement situation:

- Retirement age – when are you going to retire?
- Retirement spending – how much are you going to spend each month during retirement?
- Retirement savings – how much are you saving for retirement right now?
- Managing risk – are you taking an appropriate amount of risk with your retirement investments?

The answers to these questions will help determine if you are on track for retirement. And if someone is not on track for retirement, "pulling these levers" — or changing the answers to these questions — will help improve any retirement situation. Keep in mind: the sooner these levers are pulled, the more effect they will have on retirement.

Part Three
Tactical Retirement Considerations

Generating income in retirement and managing your cash flow.

After understanding the four levers and their appropriate use, hopefully you find yourself ready to put them to good use! Regardless of where anyone is on the path to retirement, the levers can be used to get people on track. At some point, whether it's one year or 30 years into the future, people need to figure out how to generate a "paycheck" in retirement.

Prior to retirement, people went to work and received a paycheck. Everyone has expenses and everyone has a paycheck. Over a (hopefully short) period of time, people figure out how to manage their monthly cash flow with respect to their income and expenses. Well, what happens in retirement? The paycheck stops but the expenses keep coming!

The next few sections will cover various topics related to recreating a paycheck in retirement. The topics will increase in complexity from basic to more advanced. These topics and strategies will not apply to everyone. And using "basic" topics in anyone's situation isn't a judgment, "basic" just means "it applies to most people." Some of the more advanced topics, while interesting and appropriate for some people, might be too costly or complex to implement for others. Or they might not even apply to them, and that's OK!

Where does retirement income come from?

The biggest psychological hurdle people face when starting retirement is coming to terms with not working. The biggest practical hurdle people face when starting retirement is replacing their paycheck. People work an entire career where they are concerned with saving for retirement. People climb the retirement mountain for decades before they reach the peak. Now that retirement is finally here, how do people convert your retirement savings into income at retirement?

Putting aside business owners, most people work at a job where they receive a steady paycheck. Even if there is a variable component to the income, such as overtime, a bonus, or sales commission, most people have some baseline amount of money they can count on with each paycheck. This is probably the single largest benefit to working at a job: do the work, get paid. As long as you don't get fired or the company doesn't go bankrupt, you are going to get a paycheck. People learn to be very confident in their paychecks – so much so that they will sign a long-term lease, or buy a house with a 30-year mortgage. People are very confident in their pay, and that's great because in a lot of respects, that confidence makes the economy work.

After earning a paycheck for decades, how will that paycheck be replaced? There are three main sources of retirement income:

- Retirement benefits you are eligible to receive.
- Income generated by your retirement assets.
- Withdrawals from your retirement assets.

People can have income derived from one, two, or all three of these buckets.

Retirement benefits you are eligible to receive - Social Security

The following section is taken directly from my first book, *Master Your Money*. Why is Social Security important? This is where most people derive most of their retirement income.

The United States has a social benefits program, the largest system in the world, where people pay into a program through payroll, and receive a benefit later in life. We will spend a little time looking into insurance and why one should have insurance. Social Security is another form of insurance, it is economic insurance against a reduced income in life and it also insures against running out of money should you live a very long life. People also refer to this as "social insurance." The first Social Security check was issued in 1940 and it has remained a robust factor in everyone's retirement plan since then. The purpose of Social Security is to provide benefits for retired workers, after the worker stops earning an income. There are several ways to think about Social Security and how it works. The simplest way is to think of it as a "mandatory savings" program. While you work, the federal government will collect a payroll tax through your employer. This amount, along with a matching amount from your employer, goes into your "account." It's not really an account with your name on it, but it is a notional account where the system keeps track of what you have paid in taxes throughout your career and thus, what you will receive as a benefit in the future. Over the course of your career, you will receive paychecks on a (hopefully) consistent basis, and with each paycheck, some of your earnings will be deducted and sent to the Social Security system, along with your employer's contribution. In this manner, you are being forced to save for your retirement. You have no choice in the matter because it is mandated by law. With only a few exceptions, almost entirely everyone must participate in this program. While some people do not like the "mandatory" aspect of the program, it does benefit a wide array of people who are able to accumulate a benefit for the future without having to do any planning today. Over time, you will continue to work, and pay the taxes while your benefit will continue to grow. In simple terms, the more you earn, the more you will be taxed, and therefore, the higher your benefit will be.

There are many complicated aspects to Social Security. For instance, there are 600 different ways to claim Social Security, but let's look at some of the basics. The first thing you will want to know is how to become eligible. You must work for a total of 40 quarters, or 10 years in order to qualify for benefits. Once you meet the initial requirement, the system will keep track of your earnings every year and will use the highest 35 years of earnings. Meaning if you work for 42 years, it will take the highest 35 years and drop the lowest 7. Remember that the more you earn, the more you are taxed and therefore the higher your benefit will be. The second thing you want to know is when you can start receiving your benefit. All benefits are indexed to your Full Retirement Age.

For most people who are not yet collecting, this is age 67. If you were born before 1960, it is earlier. Like we just reviewed, the system will calculate your benefit based on the highest 35 years of earnings and establish a baseline benefit at age 67. From here, you have a lot of options. If you decide to delay your benefits, your benefits will continue to increase, even if you don't work, until age 70. Beyond age 70, your benefits no longer increase. Some people call this the Latest Retirement Age. There really aren't that many reasons not to begin your benefit at age 70 as the benefit does not increase any further and at that point. You must "use it or lose it." Should you decide to begin your benefits prior to age 67, you have that option as well. As you might expect, the opposite happens. If you take your benefit prior to 67, the benefit is reduced because while the government will allow you to take the benefit before 67, they do not want to encourage you. In fact, they discourage you by decreasing the benefit. The earlier you take it, the more it is reduced. The earliest you can begin your benefit is age 62. What's important to remember is: your benefits are calculated for your Full Retirement Age, which is 67 for most people; your benefit will DECREASE if you start benefits earlier, as early as age 62; and your benefit will INCREASE if you start your benefits later, as late as age 70.

Everything just described is a summary of your Social Security, based on your earnings, work history, and when you can claim it as the recipient. The main purpose of Social Security is to provide a benefit for you at retirement. Within Social Security, there are several other programs all wrapped up into one. The first you will want to know about is the spousal benefit. For any worker who is married, the spouse is also part of the Social Security program, regardless of whether the spouse works. (The spouse is also covered even if divorced after being married for 10 years or more.) For example, if a spouse does not work, ever, for his or her entire life, the spouse can still claim a benefit based on the worker's earnings. This benefit is typically about half of the worker's benefit. And if the spouse works on his or her own record, that benefit also continues to accrue. The spouse cannot receive both, but can choose to receive the higher of the two: either the spousal benefit or their own benefit. The second program you need to know about is the survivor program. If the worker passes away, even before reaching retirement, the spouse of the deceased worker is still eligible for a benefit. In this regard, Social Security acts as a small life insurance policy that pays out in the event of your untimely death. The benefit will be paid out not only to your spouse, but also to your children if they are under 18 (19 if they are still high school students). The third program worth understanding is the disability benefit. In the event you become unable to work due to an injury or illness, and you are expected to be out of work for an extended period of time such as a year, the Social Security program will pay you a disability benefit. Therefore, this program also acts like a disability insurance program as well.

How well does this system work? It worked well for several decades but now there are a few technical challenges. Many people are living longer, which results in the benefits needing to last longer. Additionally, Social Security is funded by payroll taxes. Workers are needed to fund the system, and over time, the number of workers has decreased relative to the number of recipients. This has caused an actuarial, and political, problem. There are some difficult decisions that need to be made and it will be a politically contentious topic without doubt. Do workers working now want to pay more taxes? No! Do people receiving Social Security want their benefits to decrease?

No! Compromise will be essential to solving the problem for the long term. Is this something you should worry about? Probably. If the system is not fixed because political leaders don't do anything, the current plan is to reduce benefits across the board by 25%. If you are already receiving benefits, this will hurt. And if you are planning for future benefits, this could also hurt but less so because you have time to plan for it. This is where planning comes into play and it's important to understand where your income will come from in retirement.

Retirement benefits you are eligible to receive - pension

In addition to Social Security, many people are eligible for a pension. A pension looks and feels very similar to the Social Security program described above, except instead of the US Government administering this benefits program, your employer runs this benefit. The number of US workers who are eligible for pension benefits is small and getting smaller. The overall number of pension plans is down about 50% since 1990 and about 13% of Americans have a defined benefit pension plan.[12] But, pensions do exist and depending on your employer and how long you worked there (and how generous the program is), the pension may be a significant portion of your retirement income.

Like Social Security, there is optimization to be done as far as when you should start the benefit. Generally, the longer you wait, the higher your pension benefit will be. Typically, there are several pension options, and it is important to get a projection that details what your benefits might be, what survivor options are offered, and when the benefits will start. Once you have gathered these options, it will be much easier to make a decision in the context of a financial plan. These projections will become an important part of your plan.

Income generated by your retirement assets – dividends

There are two ways the stockowner benefits from owning shares of the stock: growth and dividends. Dividends are sort of like a paycheck for the owner. When a company reaches a certain level of profitability, the managers of the company may decide to pay some of the income to the owners. There are several factors that will determine how much, if any, the dividend payment will be. Some of them include how much total profit the company earns, the future outlook for profitability, and other investments the company can make with the cash.

So, growth and dividends are the two main reasons a person should invest in stock. If you don't think the value of the company will increase, or there is no reasonable expectation to ever receive a dividend, there's probably no reason to invest your money in this company! With these two potential sources of return, growth in the value of the company and expectation of a dividend, there come some risks.

Some of the risks of investing in stocks are obvious and some you won't know about until they punch you in the face out of nowhere. Anything that could cause the value of the company to go down would clearly be a risk because it will decrease the value of your investment, which we don't want to happen over the long term. A new competitor in the same space, a technological breakthrough that makes the business obsolete, or a change in business strategy can all cause the value of the company to decrease in various ways. These are risks specific to the company itself. There are other types of risk that will apply to all companies at the same time. This is generally called market risk. The economic cycle, current interest rates, and purchasing power are all types of risks that apply generally to all companies. And while there is not much you can do about the economic cycle, it is important to understand the financial risk you are exposing yourself to by owning shares of a company. In the worst-case scenario, if a company goes completely out of business, the stockowners typically lose all their investment. While this sounds scary, it is not so scary when you've invested in hundreds or thousands of companies at once – which is how mutual funds work. The threat of a company going out of business is very real to the owners and operators of that business, but an investor can diversify by owning hundreds or thousands of companies, thereby reducing the risk of any one company going out of business.

As a shareholder, people are entitled to a say in how the company is run, and a piece of the profits. Getting a say in how the company is run is mainly done through voting for the board of directors. It's not as if the shareholders are going to decide how to price a product, which service to offer, or what market to be in. The shareholders vote for the board of directors. And the board of directors acts as "the boss" for the CEO. So, though the CEO is "the big boss," the CEO ultimately works for the owners of the company. This concept is called corporate governance, and a full discussion is outside of the scope of this book; however, it's important to understand that "good governance" occurs when the CEO reports to an independent board of directors and is held accountable for actions and results, while "bad governance" can come in many other shapes and sizes. For example, perhaps the CEO reports to the board, and the CEO is the chairman of the board. Perhaps there are multiple family members on the board. Perhaps there are multiple share classes where the common shareholders get one vote per share and the CEO, who is also 25% owner, gets 10 votes per shares.

While getting a vote in the direction of the company is important, the main reason to own stocks for income is to receive the dividend. If the company is profitable, and over time, it must be profitable in order to remain in business, the company has to decide what to do with those profits. The company has essentially three choices: a) take the profits and reinvest in the business in the form of new products, expanded markets, acquisitions and the like; b) let the cash accumulate, which is not usually a popular decision with the shareholders; or c) distribute the profits as a dividend. Should the company decide to distribute the profits, what they will do is "declare a dividend." This dividend will be paid out to all shareholders of record as of a certain date. The dividend is distributed on a per share basis. So, if Apple declares a $3.00-per-share dividend, a person with 100 shares will receive $300 cash on the date of the dividend payment. These dividends are typically paid quarterly.

How does this translate to retirement income? First, the person seeking retirement income from dividends must search for companies that pay dividends. Remember, the companies have three choices with what to do with profits. Not all companies pay dividends. If a company is in growth mode and there are a lot of opportunities to increase business, they may not pay dividends for years. They may choose to continue expanding business with the profits. Those companies do not make good investments for retirement income! To generate retirement income, the investor must select stocks that are specifically paying dividends. The rate at which they pay dividends, which is the annual dividend divided by the stock price, is called the *dividend yield* of the stock. This is what the investor can expect to receive, on an annual basis, from the investment.

It would not be an insurmountable challenge to research and create a list of 40-50 stocks that generate dividends; however, much of that work is already done by professional investment managers. There are mutual funds and exchange traded funds that specialize in stocks that maximize dividends. For example, if an investor selects a mutual fund with a dividend yield of 4% and invests $100,000, the investor can expect approximately $4,000 per year, or $1,000 per quarter in dividend income.

Income generated by your retirement assets – bonds

The way bonds work is simple — a basic bond is a loan to the company seeking cash. The bondholder loans the company $1,000, then the company pays interest, which is called the coupon. This is typically paid twice per year. If this is a 10-year bond, the company will pay interest two times per year for 10 years, then after the 10-year period, the company will return the $1,000 loaned by the bondholder. Why would someone loan money to a company? The interest payment that is received twice per year can be used as income. Keep in mind: a bond is less risky than a stock, so people can rely on this interest payment as a source of income. There are several parameters for bonds as an investment, the main ones being: maturity, quality of the bond (creditworthiness of the company), and the type of loan. Maturity is a fancy way to say the length of time of the loan. Some loans can be very short, as short as overnight and some can be very long. In today's environment, 30 years is considered a long maturity, but some bonds can be as long as 50 or 100 years.

The quality of the bond is a way referring to the strength of the credit rating for the issuer. Just like when you apply for a mortgage, a stronger credit rating will result in a lower interest rate. The mortgage company has faith you will pay your mortgage. Similarly, the bond holder has faith in a quality company's ability to pay the coupon. It's important to understand the credit rating for the bond you are investing in. While it may seem appealing to receive a higher interest rate, you may be taking additional, unnecessary risk. The higher the interest rate, the higher the likelihood of default.

The final parameter to understand is the type of bond and who is issuing it. The main categories of issuers are companies (corporate bonds), the federal government (treasury bonds), and local governments (municipal bonds). All these factors are woven into a patchwork of the bond being offered, which is boiled down to how much risk the investor is taking and what is the potential reward.

Just like stocks, there are thousands of bonds to choose from. Similarly, there is the choice of investing in individual bonds, or into a mutual fund or exchange traded fund of bonds. And again, it would not be an insurmountable task to create a bond portfolio of 40-50 bonds; however, it is typically easier, and less risky, to select an appropriate bond fund through either a mutual fund or exchange traded fund. How does this translate into retirement income? The main purpose of this investment is to generate income in the form of coupon payments. Most bonds are issued for a certain period of time, ranging from 1-2 months to 30 years. And over this time period, the investor will receive interest payments, typically every six months. For example, if an investor invests $100,000 in a bond with a 5% interest, or coupon rate, the investor can expect to receive $5,000, or $2,500 two times per year.

Income generated by your retirement assets – guaranteed income from annuities

Another way to generate income with your retirement assets is to use an annuity. Annuities are a potentially controversial topic. Consider being skeptical of anyone who has a strong opinion about annuities, either for or against. An annuity is a tool, it is neither good nor bad. Just like a hammer is neither good nor bad, it's just a tool. If you need to bang in a nail, a hammer is a pretty great tool. If you need to paint a room, a hammer is practically useless. A person who believes an annuity is appropriate for anyone, in any situation, at any time is probably... wait for it... an annuity salesperson. A person who believes an annuity is never appropriate, under any circumstances, probably doesn't have a full appreciation for how an annuity works or how it can benefit a certain set of people.

You might want to ask, "But don't annuities have really high fees?" Well, this is partially true. Yes, annuities contain embedded fees. And yes, these fees are probably higher than a low-cost mutual fund or ETF. But why do these fees exist? What is the benefit of an annuity? Why would anyone use an annuity?

Annuities are a great way to guarantee income for the rest of your life. A person will carve out a piece of their retirement assets, usually no more than 50% of their total retirement assets, and then they'll transfer those dollars into a contract with an annuity company. In exchange for transferring these dollars, the insurance company will guarantee a set income stream, usually paid monthly, for the rest of the person's life. This solves two problems: first, the person no longer needs to worry about "outliving the money." The income stream is guaranteed for life, so a person with high longevity doesn't have to worry about running out of money. You can think of this as "longevity insurance." The second problem it solves is partially relieving some of the asset management. Rather than worry about investment performance, asset allocation, and monthly withdrawals, the annuity pays out a fixed amount every month, thus eliminating some of this investment management.

Since there is no such thing as a free lunch, the significant benefits described come at a cost, the first cost being the fees embedded in the annuity product. Due to these costs, and the nature of annuity investments, your overall rate of return on this part of your retirement assets will most likely be lower than the remainder of your portfolio if it is invested in a moderately aggressive asset allocation. But this trade off will be worth it for the person looking to receive a fixed amount of guaranteed income. The second drawback is that this money is no longer liquid. Depending on the exact annuity product and the terms and conditions of the product, the money could be completely illiquid, meaning it is never accessible, or illiquid for a defined period of time. Like any insurance product, there is a lot of "fine print" to review. Be sure to fully understand all aspects of any insurance contract before entering it.

Are annuities for everyone, at any time, in any situation? No! An annuity solves a problem: a person wishes to receive income from the investment but does not want to experience market risk. Depending on the circumstances, it may make sense to transfer some of your retirement assets to an annuity contract to ensure you have some level of guaranteed income. Many annuity investors consider this to be their "paycheck." Psychologically, many millions of people can manage to accumulate $500,000 or even $1,000,000 into a retirement plan. Once established, the "saving" part of life can be quite simple. If it comes out of the paycheck or bank account automatically, people can "set it and forget it." Once that money is accumulated, it can be difficult psychologically to begin withdrawing these funds. And not only is it a challenge psychologically, but now those people must consider *when* to make withdrawals, from *which funds* to make withdrawals, and *how much* to withdraw. This can be a complex challenge without the help of a professional. One way to simplify this management is to use an annuity, at least for part of the assets. The annuity will convert the amount invested into an *income stream*, or what most people refer to as a paycheck. Managing a $500,000 IRA with the various investments, withdrawals, and performance can be a challenge. Receiving a check for $2,000 per month is a breeze. While yes, there is a small cost to using this product, it not only resolves the challenges of managing a paycheck, it also removes most if not all of the market risk and also protects against spending down the funds. People can outlive or outspend a $500,000 IRA, but they cannot outspend $2,000 per month for life.

Withdrawals from your retirement assets – the 4% rule

In addition to income received from various sources of retirement benefits, people also have the ability to draw on assets saved for retirement. This is where people tap into their 401(k), IRA, 403(b), Roth IRAs, and any other qualified retirement account after many years of diligently saving for retirement. People ask:

- How do I know how much to withdraw?
- How do I know if I'll run out of money?
- Is it OK to withdraw extra money this year to install a new roof or take a big trip?

It may be beneficial to review these questions with a financial advisor. A financial advisor will have access to financial planning software that can model your retirement in terms of assets and cash flow. As previously discussed, a professional can model spending in the "go-go" years, the "slow-go" years, and the "no-go" years with long-term care costs.

In addition to using the fancy software to give you confidence in your retirement plan, the advisor may explain "The 4% Rule." This basic rule of thumb says to withdraw no more than 3-5% of your retirement assets in any given year. You may also see this as the "3% rule" or the "5% rule." There are many studies both supporting and disproving of this rule, which is why it is not a guarantee for success, but more like a loose guideline. There are many factors affecting retirement projections: inflation, asset rates of return, actual spending levels, and longevity to name a few. These factors are all ingredients of a thick stew referred to as "retirement." And the best thing to do is get professional help with financial planning software to review your retirement plan annually. But on the scale between getting professional help and doing nothing lies the 4% rule.

The math is not complicated. In any given year, limit your asset withdrawal to approximately 3-5% of the balance, so we'll use 4% as an average.

- Sam's 401(k) - $250,000
- Sally's IRA - $250,000
- Total Retirement Assets - $500,000
- 4% of $500,000 is $20,000

So, in the current year, Sam and Sally should feel pretty confident withdrawing $20,000. This will leave them with $480,000 and depending on market performance, their assets may increase or decrease from that point. To continue the example:

- Total Retirement Assets after withdrawals - $480,000
- Market performance of 3% - $14,400
- New Retirement Assets - $494,400
- 4% of $494,400 is $19,776

Depending on market performance, they may be able to draw more or less than the $20,000 withdrawn in the first year. For all the math nerds out there, you may notice if the rate of return is consistently above 4%, their account balances will actually *increase* even after withdrawing 4%. And for all the *really big* math nerds out there, you may wish to argue that the withdrawals will come out monthly, and the performance will vary within the year. Fair point, but this is a simplified example. The principle is correct even if the actual results vary.

Taking these withdrawals in the context of changing account values due to market fluctuation can become stressful. Remember the adage "buy low and sell high," and if the market is down 10%, 20%, or 40%, it will be a psychological challenge to sell some investments to make withdrawals. One technique to eliminate at least some of this volatility is to "carve out" the amount to be withdrawn from the investment portfolio and hold it as cash. Continuing the example above, if Sam and Sally have $500,000 and they wish to withdraw $20,000 per year each year, they might start out with the following asset allocation:

- 60% stocks, or approximately $300,000
- 40% bonds, or approximately $200,000

And then using the "carve out" strategy, they might conservatively carve out 24 months of withdrawals, or approximately $40,000, thus making their allocation:

- 8% cash, or approximately $40,000
- 56% stocks, or approximately $280,000
- 36% bonds, or approximately $180,000

Now Sam and Sally have set aside the amount of cash they are going to withdraw over the next 24 months, so no matter what the stock market or bond market does, whether the markets perform well or not, they can rest assured they have the cash available to withdraw. Then over time, they can continue to monitor investment performance, make adjustments to their asset allocation, and replenish the cash they withdraw. Some people use stock dividends or bond interest to replenish the cash allocation. Since they are continually withdrawing cash, it is helpful to use the income from stocks or bonds to "top off" the account with cash.

Withdrawals from your retirement assets – required minimum distributions

If the question "how much can I withdraw?" is on one end of a spectrum, on the other end of the spectrum sits the question "how much *must* I withdraw?" Yes, that's correct, there comes a time where withdrawals are required. This is known as the required minimum distribution, or RMD for short. This applies to any tax-deferred retirement account. To review, this is the 401(k), IRA, 403(b), SIMPLE IRA, SEP IRA, and others. This is the first leg of the triangle.

Remember how these accounts work: the owner contributes to these accounts on a tax-deferred basis. That is, the money contributed to these accounts are *deducted* from income in the year of the contribution, thus, taxes are not yet paid. They are *deferred*. And that deferral, while a huge tax benefit to the owner, is a huge tax detriment to the United States Treasury. Every dollar the owner defers in taxes is a dollar Uncle Sam cannot spend. So, the IRS lets this party go on for years and years, decades even. Then at some point, the IRS says to the owners: "OK, party is over. It's time to withdraw the money so you can finally pay some taxes on it."

When is the party over? It depends on your birthday because tax law in the 2020s made some changes. For the longest time, these required distributions began at age 70.5 (don't ask why — no idea!). Then changes allowed some people to wait until 72, and then 73, and eventually 75. The minimum distributions still apply to everyone, but the age at which they begin will change based on your birth year.

And like any good government program, there are penalties! It's important to take these required distributions because the penalty for not taking them is a percentage of the untaken amount. So, you may as well take the distribution because if you don't, you'll end up giving a large chunk of money to the United States Treasure, in *addition* to the taxes you owe!

Budget

Here's a section no one will want to read but should! Budgeting is not a lot of fun; however, it is a key component to successfully managing personal finances. Without a budget, the situation can get out of hand pretty quickly. What exactly is a budget? It is essentially a plan for your monthly spending. This is a major step toward putting the *planning* into *financial planning*.

There are two approaches you can take. Well, there are three if you include the strategy of completely winging it! This is not recommended, but people do it. There are probably some months where this strategy is fun, but there are many, many months where this is very stressful. On a personal note, I can attest that spending more than your income is very stressful. I know from experience.

So, let's all agree we aren't going to wing it. That leaves us with two options: we can make our budget from the "top-down" or the "bottom-up." "Top down" starts with income and work to arrive at what can be spent each month. "Bottom up" starts at identifying what is spent each month and work backwards to the income. There is no right or wrong way to do it, as long as you create your budget and stick to it. Regardless of which method you choose, you will have to go through a couple of iterations to make sure it is reasonable and manageable.

If you prefer to go from the "top-down," you would start with your income. How much money do you have coming in from your sources of income? This would include your salary, your spouse's salary, and any other income you can rely on each month. If you are retired, this would include Social Security, pensions, annuities, and anything else consistent. We will address investment income and withdrawals at a later time. This income would not include any bonus you may or may not receive, one-time events that occur in life, inheritances, or even inconsistent overtime pay. You want this number to be *realistic* and *reliable*. If we can't rely on the income amount, it will make budgeting very difficult. Once you've identified your income, you will need to account for taxes to arrive at your net income. This is what you need to spend each month. For example:

The Four Levers

- $5,000 per month Sam's income
- $5,000 per month, Sally's income
- $10,000 total gross income
- $2,000 federal taxes (estimate)
- $500 state taxes (estimate)
- $800 payroll taxes (estimate)
- This leaves $6,700 net This is what you're left with to spend!

After arriving at your net income, you can start to make a plan for how you are going to spend this money. Start with what's called your *fixed expenses*. The primary fixed expenses are housing, either the mortgage or rent, property taxes, various insurance premiums, and any other debt payments such as student loans or auto loans. Don't forget your savings. Maybe you participate in your workplace retirement plan and retirement savings comes out of your paycheck. That's great because you've already accounted for your retirement savings in the net income. But if not, you will also want to include in the fixed expenses any systematic savings you are doing. These are the expenses you absolutely must pay every month, and they stay relatively the same each month.

Once you have covered your fixed expenses, you will need to account for your *variable expenses*. These are a different set of expenses that you must cover each month, but the amount is not necessarily the same month-to-month. This can be a little more difficult to manage and you'll have to assume what this amount will be each month. Most people have utility bills, transportation, and food as variable expenses they must cover each month.

What's left over is reserved for *discretionary spending*. After going through the boring budget, here's the first chance to have fun with the money! Since we started with our net income and then accounted for our fixed and variable expenses, as long as we have already accounted for our retirement savings either as a payroll deduction or fixed expense, we can spend our discretionary money guilt-free.

To summarize how to make a top-down budget:

- Start with gross income from all sources, then account for what gets deducted to arrive at your net income.
- Subtract out fixed expenses, including retirement savings if not already deducted.
- Subtract out variable expenses, making an educated guess on the average amount they will be.
- Whatever is left over is for discretionary expenses; spend it guilt-free!

The other way to do a budget is to go from the bottom up. Here, you can start with a list of the various items people spend money on. You can download a detailed budget from any number of websites, or you can make your own. The Federal Trade Commission has a good one[13]. Once you have a complete listing, start filling in the details.

Begin with your known fixed expenses. This is the same activity described above, just in a little different order. List out your rent or mortgage, debt payments, and any other fixed expenses. And don't forget to include your retirement savings, whether it is coming out of your pay or you are saving on a regular basis. After that, fill in the details on your variable expenses. It's helpful to use a monthly average on these items. Keep going down your budget items to make assumptions on your discretionary expenses. This is where the bottom-up method is drastically different than the top-down method because the first method asks "What can you spend given your income?" and this method asks "How does what I am actually spending compare to my income?" Using the top-down method, the discretionary spending is what is left over. The bottom-up method uses the budget worksheet to make an estimate on what you spend on discretionary items. Be honest and don't lie to yourself!

After completing the budget worksheet where you detail the fixed expenses, variable expenses, and discretionary expenses, the next step is to compare this to your net income. And here is where you may need to iterate the entire process to arrive at a good budget. If your total spending is less than your net income, great! As long as you were truthful in your spending habits, you should have money left over at the end of the month. You can use this money to increase your savings, or possibly increase your spending if you feel that is appropriate. If your total spending is more than your net income, that's OK! It may be necessary to review your spending a few times to make sure you are accurate in your assumptions. After you review the budget *on paper,* review the budget *in real life*. Here are some indicators you may be spending more than your income each month:

- You have accumulated, and continue to accumulate, credit card debt.
- You never seem to have enough money for discretionary spending.
- You aren't saving any money.
- There is never any money left over in your account after you pay all your bills.
- You feel stressed.

If one or more of these apply to you, it could be the case you are spending more than your income. It would be a lot less stressful if you changed this situation! Once you confirm you are spending more than your income, both in your budget and in real life, the most important step is to take action to reduce your spending. There are books written about this subject – how to prioritize what you spend your money on. To keep it simple, your fixed expenses are fixed for a reason – you probably need to pay your rent and your car payment! While that is true, perhaps you can live in a cheaper place. Or you can reduce your discretionary spending. The advice "make your coffee at home" has become sort of a cliché. Let's be honest, buying a latte at Starbucks is probably not the reason you are not a billionaire. But, if you are constantly overspending your income each month, while at the same time spending $4 per day on a Frappuccino, that's $120 per month you can knock off your budget if it helps you. It's all about priorities.

To summarize the bottom-up approach:

- List out your fixed and variable expenses – what you need to pay for each month.
- Don't forget to include your retirement savings.
- List out your discretionary expenses – make good estimates and be honest.
- Total your spending and compare it to your net income.
- If your total spending is less than your income, great! Keep that level of spending.
- If your total spending is more than your income, go back and verify the numbers.
- After you verify the numbers and your results are the same, then you must start the hard work of finding out areas to reduce your spending.

- Keep working until your spending is less than your income.

Once you've gone through the (hopefully not too painful) exercise of getting your total monthly spending down to less than your income, here are a few tips to make the process of managing your spending as easy as possible.

First, maintain a budget worksheet. This can be done on a phone app, through a website, or a good old-fashioned spreadsheet. There are tons and tons of free options, so this is not an area where you should be spending $19 per month for a budgeting app. Maintaining this budgeting worksheet is what used to be called "balancing your checkbook." You'll want to look at this every so often to make sure you have enough money in your checking account.

Unless you are really "old school," very few people are writing checks to pay the bills. Whether the bills are fixed like your rent or mortgage, or variable like your electric bill, it's very convenient to have these bills come out of your account electronically. If you think back to the top-down budgeting, start with your net income, then subtract out your fixed and variable items, and you are left with your discretionary budget. The simplest way to manage your discretionary budget is to get one credit card and put all your discretionary spending on it. Then you can download the credit card app on your phone, and every so often, you can check the balance on the app. It's easy math to come up with your discretionary budget; then divide by 4 to arrive at your weekly spending budget. With a few touches on your phone, you can keep up to date with how much you have spent so far each day, week, or month.

A word of caution on the credit card: only use a credit card if you have the discipline to monitor your spending and maintain your spending at or below your planned budget! Credit cards are very convenient and when used appropriately, they are a great way to borrow money for 3-4 weeks at 0% interest. But, and this is a huge "but," if you do not use the credit card appropriately, the banks will eat your lunch. The top four banks in the United States typically earn tens of billions of dollars in profits each year. You will buy that $4 latte and it will end up costing you $11 to pay it off over 10 years (not an exaggeration — you can do the math with a basic amortization calculation). Do this a few hundred times per year and you are setting yourself up for financial stress.

If you are confident in your ability to control your spending, stick to your discretionary budget, pay off the credit card each month (thus not paying any interest to the bank), and then find one with the best rewards. Maybe you like having the cash put back on your card, or maybe you like to line up free airline travel. Whatever your preference, as long as you are paying the balance off each month, it's well worth some research to find the best rewards credit card. This will pay some dividends on something you have to do anyway – pay for all your junk!

Chapter 5
More advanced topics

Managing taxable income

Perhaps one of the most overlooked concepts, and the most substantial reason to work with a financial advisor, is managing taxable income in retirement. Crossing over to retirement is a mindset shift in how to think about taxes. During the working years, taxes are the result of income. And most of the people, most of the time as they move through their careers, are in the game of maximizing their income. And as income is maximized, taxes will increase. Yes, there are strategies and tactics to minimize taxes for any given level of income, but there are only so many strategies available and so many ways in which to employ them. So generally, as people's income increases throughout their careers, their taxes will also increase.

The mindset shift required for thinking about taxes in retirement presents itself in two ways. First, rather than maximizing income, which is what most people do over most of their careers, the goal is generating as little income as possible while maintaining your desired lifestyle. Minimizing income will minimize taxes, all other factors being equal. This is the exact opposite of what most people do while working, thus a significant difference.

The second mindset shift required is to understand the various sources of retirement income and how they impact the tax liability in any given year. Again, this is a drastic change. Most people throughout their careers work at a job or are self-employed. Aside from the various deductions and exclusions available in the tax filing process, people are taxed on substantially all income. The average effective tax rate of households earning $100,000 is about 18-20%. And this "typical" household earning $100,000 gross probably has a marginal tax rate of 12%, meaning if the household earns an additional $2,000, $240 of that $2,000 will be taxed. This is assuming a gross income of $100,000 with a household of two income earners has a $24,000 standard deduction, thus making their taxable income $76,000 and their marginal tax bracket 12% as of 2023. This is neither good nor bad, it just *is*. While it can be a bummer that the additional income will be taxed at this rate, it is very simple to understand and manage. In fact, no planning or thought is required. If a person makes additional money, additional taxes will be withheld and most likely no other actions will need to be taken.

Contrast this with the idea that different sources of retirement income are taxed differently. While this ultimately means the overall tax liability is probably lower, there is a lot more to understand and manage. Refer back to the tax control triangle section to refresh your mind on how different accounts are taxed at withdrawal. Here is a summary of various sources of retirement income and how they are taxed:

Retirement Income Source	How is it taxed?	Comments
Social Security	If total income is below a certain level, Social Security is not taxed. Above certain levels, up to 85% of the Social Security benefit is taxable.	This is the main source of retirement income for most people.
Pensions	Generally taxable.	This is becoming less and less prevalent over time.
IRA, 401(k), 403(b) withdrawals	Generally taxable.	Subject to RMDs (required minimum distributions).
Roth IRA, Roth 401(k), Roth 403(b) withdrawals	Generally not taxable.	Generally, if withdrawals are made after age 59.5 and after holding for 5 years, the earnings are tax free.
Non-qualified account withdrawals	Only capital gains on the asset are taxed.	Taxes are due in the year the assets are sold.
Checking, savings, money market withdrawals	Generally not taxable	Taxes are due as interest is paid each year; thus any future withdrawals are tax-free.

How do these potential streams of income in retirement compare to the typical paycheck? Managing the taxes on these income streams is much more complicated. But in these complications lies an opportunity: the opportunity to control, at least to some extent, a person's income in any given taxable year. Think about it: if a person has substantial assets in a Roth IRA, Roth 401(k), or a savings account, any withdrawals are generally not taxable. So, if the person can live off the withdrawals for one year, the income in that given year will be exactly $0. This may or may not be practical based on the lifestyle spending for that person, or the asset level in these accounts, but this example serves as an illustration of the principle: different retirement income sources are taxed differently.

What must be true in order to control retirement income? There needs to be a variety of retirement income sources.

With a variety of income sources, the person has greater control over the exact amount of taxable income. To give another example, if this same person, instead of withdrawing money from a Roth IRA, Roth 401(k), or savings account, withdraws the same amount of money to cover the same level of spending from a Traditional IRA or 401(k), 100% of those withdrawals will be taxable.

Having some assets in each of these retirement income sources will give more flexibility in controlling retirement income and therefore taxes paid. As discussed earlier, the more time available for planning, the more impact a person can have on retirement planning. If a person is *at or nearing* retirement, there may not be much opportunity to balance the triangle. And that's OK! The more time available until retirement, the more opportunity to take different actions to diversify retirement income streams.

Cash value life insurance

Life insurance products get a bad rap. This is very similar to the annuity situation. Life insurance is a tool. It is neither good nor bad. Go to a life insurance firm and they will sell you life insurance! While that may be unfortunate is some situations, that does not make the product bad.

Life insurance comes in two basic forms: term and permanent. Some people will call permanent life insurance "cash value" life insurance for reasons that will hopefully become clear in a few hundred words. Term life insurance is really "death" insurance. It works just like car insurance, which should be called "accident" insurance. A person pays a premium to a car insurance firm, and in the unlikely event the person gets into an accident, the insurance company will pay to repair the car and hospitalize anyone injured. It is pure insurance: pay a premium, and if some bad event happens, the insurance pays a benefit. This is called risk transfer; most drivers do not wish to carry the risk of destroying their car, another person's car, all while racking up potentially hundreds of thousands of dollars in medical bills. Seems like a no brainer to transfer that risk to an insurance company for $100 to $200 per month, and yet people don't do it! So many people are resistant to this idea that almost all states *require* you to buy car insurance, and even specify how much and the type of insurance people must carry.

Term life insurance works the same way. Pay a premium, and assuming you are healthy (it is very difficult-to-impossible to get life insurance if you are not well), in the unlikely event the person dies in the next 1, 5, 10, or 20 years, someone will get a benefit. The person decides how much the benefit is. It could be as low as $5,000 or $10,000 to cover funeral expenses, or it could be millions of dollars.

What does this have to do with retirement? Not much! Term life insurance is a product that may or may not be appropriate for your situation and is less relevant for retirement than permanent insurance. There are strategies involving permanent life insurance that can be used in retirement. In contrast with term life insurance, permanent life insurance has two components. First, there is an insurance component that looks and feels an awful lot like term insurance. For all practical purposes, it is just like term insurance. Pay a premium, get a benefit at death. The second component is drastically different, and it is much like an investment account linked to the insurance policy. In addition to the insurance component and premium, there will be an additional component and premium that is essentially an investment account. This is called the "cash value" component of the policy but it is not necessarily held as cash.

Depending on the policy, the cash value component can be invested in assets such as stocks and bonds, just like an Individual Retirement Account or 401(k). The policy owner continues to pay premiums, some of which go to the insurance component and some of which go to the investment component. Just like the 401(k) and IRA, over a long enough time horizon, the market has returned 6-10% on average.

This becomes another vehicle to save for retirement. Generally speaking, when set up the right way, it can fall into the Tax-Free leg of the triangle. While this can be a major benefit, it's important to note this appears toward the end of this book and not the beginning. This is not the preferred vehicle, by any stretch. But it has some great applications. The main situations where a permanent life insurance policy is most applicable are typically with high earners. High earners can run into two problems when saving for retirement. Retirement savings plans all have contribution limits. So, depending on a person's income and available cash flow, the person may contribute the maximum amount to a retirement plan and still seek out opportunities to save for retirement. Once all these plans have been maximized, a permanent life insurance policy may be an appropriate place to save. In addition to contribution limits, many retirement plans have income limits. Roth IRAs have very straightforward income limits. If income is above a certain amount, no contributions are allowed. Depending on the size of your company and how the 401(k) is set up, certain high-income individuals may have their participation in the 401(k) limited. Here lies another opportunity to save into a permanent policy.

Use a line of credit to manage cash flow and sequence of return issues

Debt can be a controversial topic for a number of reasons, and it is classically categorized as "good" or "bad" debt. Books have been written about the use of debt, and more importantly, how to eliminate it. One of the less common uses of debt is to establish a home equity line of credit for retirement. A home equity line of credit, or HELOC, can be used in a few different ways. There are the classic uses of a HELOC such as purchasing a vehicle or making home improvements. The benefit of using the HELOC here is getting a generally more favorable interest rate since the loan is collateralized by the house. The other benefit is using these funds to make the purchase and paying it off over time, instead of withdrawing from retirement savings to make the purchase.

In addition to the standard uses of a line of credit, there are additional uses specifically in retirement. The first use is to replace an emergency fund. It's prudent to keep three to six months of expenses set aside in case of an emergency. In retirement, a retiree can't lose their job practically by definition, but emergencies will still arise. Roofs will leak, water tanks will break, and cars will need repairs. Rather than tie up a significant amount of cash, opening a line of credit will allow access to cash without keeping cash on the sidelines. Then in the case of emergency, the cash is available, and interest will be due only on the amount used. In the worst-case scenario, the funds used to cover an emergency will accrue some interest until it's paid back. And in the best-case scenario, rather than setting aside cash for an emergency, which will not see much in the way of interest or growth, the cash can remain invested along with the other retirement funds, hopefully growing over this time.

The second, and more advanced, use of a line of credit in retirement is to help smooth out withdrawals in times when account values are down due to market performance. Remember the mantra "Buy low, and sell high"? Well, in retirement, people are almost always net sellers. And people in retirement want to "sell high"! But selling high isn't always possible when the market is down for whatever reason. And selling is essentially a requirement throughout retirement because the assets need to be sold in order to fund lifestyle spending. One way to mitigate the impact of this is to use a line of credit. In times when the markets are down, draw on the line of credit for a period of time. Then, if the market goes back up, the line of credit can be paid off and there will be additional funds available (because the market has gone up). This is a more advanced strategy and may be difficult or cumbersome to manage independently. This strategy is most suitable as part of a comprehensive financial plan with a professional.

Qualified charitable distributions

Qualified charitable distributions, or QCDs, are a way to "kill two birds with one stone." A QCD is a donation to charity that is conducted in a very particular way. QCDs apply to people who are subject to the Required Minimum Distribution requirement and as a tax law change in the 2020s, you can actually make a QCD at age 70 ½ , even if you are not yet subject to Required Minimum Distributions. Remember how the Required Minimum Distribution, or RMD, works: once a person reaches a certain age, which could be 70 ½, 72, 73, or 75 depending on a person's birthday,

US Treasury rules *require* that a certain amount of money is withdrawn from qualified plans each year. These qualified plans include IRA, 401(k), 403(b), and generally anything considered "pre-tax."

Here is how the QCD "kills two birds with one stone." The required minimum distribution is taken from the pre-tax account such as an IRA and donated to charity. Here's the first bird, the person made a charitable donation. And then, as long as the donation is done in a certain way, that donation becomes tax deductible, therefore negating the taxable income generated by the IRA distribution. Since the IRA account is "pre-tax" and "tax-deferred," any money distributed from the IRA becomes taxable income. But, in the case of the QCD, because it is donated to charity, the distribution in this case is not taxable.

But aren't charitable donations tax deductible anyway? Yes and no. It will depend on the tax law at any given point and it's difficult to generalize the tax law based on the tax law at any specific point in time. Historically speaking, a nominal amount of charitable donation is typically deductible on the tax return, even without itemizing. This could be a few hundred dollars. Anything above that amount typically requires the taxpayer to *itemize* tax deductions on the form Schedule A. While it's not a major issue to fill out this form, the game within the game of itemizing deductions is to compare the taxpayer's potential itemized deductions with the standard deduction. Depending on the tax law at any given point, the standard deduction may be relatively high, or it may be relatively low. In times where it is relatively low, itemizing deductions becomes more beneficial to do with the lower threshold. In the case where the standard deduction is higher, the taxpayer must have significant itemized deductions in order to meet the threshold. For example, in

2023, the standard deduction is $13,850 for a single person and $27,700 for a couple filing jointly. This means a married couple would need to have total itemized deductions, including mortgage interest, state income tax, and local taxes in addition to the charitable deductions *above* $26,000 in order for it to make sense to itemize.

What does this all mean? Let's go back to the original question: Aren't charitable deductions tax deductible anyway? In the case of a couple filing jointly, with no mortgage interest, $4,000 in state taxes, and $4,000 in local taxes, they would need to donate more than $18,000 to charity to itemize their deductions. So, if this couple graciously and generously donates $10,000 to charity, the donation is essentially not deductible, because they would use the standard deduction when filing.

This is where the QCD strategy for people at or beyond RMD age becomes very beneficial; the QCD strategy does not require itemized deductions for the tax filing. Since the donation is treated separately as a QCD, it is not taxable, thus eliminating the need to itemize deductions. The higher the standard deduction in any given year, the more relevant this strategy will be. And it's worth noting that as of the time of this writing, the QCD strategy has an annual maximum of $100,000. For example, Sam and Sally, age 75:

- rent their home (no mortgage interest deduction).
- pay $2,000 in state taxes.
- have no medical expenses.
- take their $10,000 required minimum distribution.
- gift $10,000 to charity

Given these facts, their total itemized deductions would be $12,000 ($2,000 state taxes plus $10,000 charitable deduction) but their standard deduction would be $27,700, meaning it would be more beneficial to claim the standard deduction than the itemized deductions and the $10,000 IRA distribution to meet the Required Minimum Distribution would be taxable. But, since they have a Required Minimum Distribution between the two of them of $10,000, instead of taking the distribution then donating the cash to charity, they could coordinate a Qualified Charitable Distribution to be paid directly from the IRA(s) to the charity. When done properly, this donation to charity will do two things: first, it will satisfy the Required Minimum Distribution and second, it will not count as taxable income. This is a great way to satisfy the desire to contribute to charity while minimizing the tax burden to the greatest extend possible.

Long-term care

A potential problem area with regards to medical spending is long-term care. Some people may call this assisted living or nursing home care. There is a wide array of potential options in this area, ranging from full service, top of the line care to having a medical professional come to the house.

The overall cost for this range of options is significant and will obviously throw a wrench in even the most finely tuned financial plan. Unfortunately, there are no good answers to magically make this problem go away. Here are three OK-but-not-great answers and their pros and cons.

First, you could take the potential cost of long-term care into account during your retirement planning. Depending on the total retirement assets available, this may or may not be feasible. The average monthly cost of long-term care, in a nursing home with a private room in 2023 is about $9,000 per month. A four year stay at a facility of this nature would cost roughly $432,000. Again, depending on the total amount of assets available, this may be a significant percentage of the total assets, which would therefore have a terrible impact on any retirement plan.

Another option would be purchasing long-term care insurance. This is another OK-but-not-great answer because the cost of the insurance is also very high. And many people do not enjoy the "use-or-lose" aspect of long-term care insurance. In the unfortunate event of suddenly dying at home without ever using a long-term care facility, after dutifully paying long-term care premiums for one or two decades, this product and all the premiums, would be essentially "lost." No one likes that idea. On the flip side, should the insured require long-term care in the future, at least some portion of the bill would be covered.

The final option, which may be the best option but not necessarily the cheapest one, is to use what's called a hybrid policy. What is it a hybrid of? A permanent life insurance policy plus an option to cover long-term care costs while the insured is alive. This option on the insurance contract will be a small fraction of a pure long-term care insurance policy; however, the underlying permanent insurance needs to be funded. This may make sense and be very cost-effective if there is a need for the permanent policy. If there is little need or desire for the permanent life insurance policy, this is another OK-but-not-great solution for long-term care costs.

In many sections of this book, "the answer" is given, this is not one of those sections. There are a good number of solutions for long-term care costs and none of them are great. What each individual chooses to do should involve family, loved ones, a financial advisor, and possibly an estate planning attorney. A good decision is possible only after consulting with all these people.

Annual gifting

Some people, as they make their way through retirement, realize they actually have enough money to sustain themselves throughout retirement and maybe even some extra. They are then faced with the decision of what to do with the extra. In his book *Die With Zero*, Bill Perkins argues it is better to give your money away while alive and able to witness the joy of giving than it is to leave money to heirs at death. This is a great point and worthy of consideration, although it can be difficult to determine across various retirement assets what will be "needed" versus what will be "extra."

Assuming a person is even able to determine what will be extra, making them a potential candidate for gifting, it may make sense to give some of these assets away while alive. And because it is a simple fact of life that any financial transaction involves taxes in some respect, here is a basic overview of some gifting strategies.

The first thing to understand about the tax consequences of gifting is anyone can give a gift to any one person up to a certain amount without any tax implications. In 2023, this amount is $17,000 and is periodically adjusted for inflation. It's worth noting this is an annual amount and it is per person. Meaning in 2023, Sam can give his son $17,000, tax-free. He can also give $17,000 to each of his nine grandchildren tax-free, for a total tax-free gift of $170,000 across 10 people in this one given year. He could do the same next year, and the year after, assuming the tax laws don't change. And if Sam is married to Sally, Sally could use the same strategy, giving $17,000 to the same son and the same nine grandchildren. They could each give $17,000 to the same person, all tax-free. Now obviously, Sam and Sally need to determine that this money is "extra" and verify they do not anticipate needing this hypothetical gift of $340,000. If this is the case, then they are in a great position for retirement!

What happens above this amount? That answer can get complicated, and a full analysis and explanation are outside the scope of this book. The short answer is that these gifts will continue to be tax-free, up to a certain point which is well above $10,000,000 in 2023. Gifts in between the $17,000 and $10,000,000 (that's quite a wide range!) will generally be tax-free, although such gifts will require an accountant and some paperwork. Another consideration is that below the $17,000 threshold, the tax-free gift can be an annual occurrence without any tax implications. But above the $17,000 threshold, the gifts become a *cumulative* event and once the $10,000,000 threshold is breached, taxes will be triggered and payable. Anyone considering giving gifts above $17,000 should consider consulting with a financial professional such as an accountant.

Conclusion

What if I'm not on track?

You're not on track? Congratulations! The first step toward *getting on track* is figuring this out. Here's a good opportunity to engage the help of a professional. About a dozen analogies could be inserted here; the main idea is that while it will cost money to get professional help, that money is almost always well worth it. There are times to fix a leaky sink yourself, and there are times to call a plumber. The plumber charges a set rate based on the skills and experiences gained practicing the craft of plumbing. Not only will the plumber get the job done in less time than the weekend warrior, it will be done the right way. Yes, the plumber costs money, but it's almost always cheaper in the long run to have it done right the first time.

Conclusion

If continuing to "do it yourself" is the only way to go for whatever reason, think back to the four levers:

1. Retire later.
2. Spend less.
3. Save more.
4. Take more risk if it's appropriate.

If you've decided to get professional help, the best course of action is to interview a few different financial advisors. If you prefer to meet someone in person, stick to the local area. If you are open to meeting virtually, search from coast to coast. It's important to work with someone you like and someone you trust. You will be spending a lot of time with this person and sharing all your personal details with them. Here are some questions to ask an advisor:

• How are you compensated?

   ◇ Great answers: fee-based, fee-only, flat fee, percentage of assets, hourly rate.

   ◇ Not great answers: commission only on products sold.

• When in our relationship are you acting as a fiduciary? When are you not?

   ◇ Great answers: always a fiduciary, a fiduciary in this case but not this case.

   ◇ Not great answers: never a fiduciary, what's a fiduciary?

Conclusion

• How much do you charge for financial planning?

◇ Great answer: any reasonable fee in your budget – 1-2% of your income is a good rule of thumb.

◇ Not great answer: we don't charge for planning (usually because we either do not have a comprehensive financial planning offering, or we are trying to sell you products).

• What conflicts of interest exist in our relationship?

◇ Great answer: We have this legitimate conflict with a reasonable explanation.

◇ Not great answer: We have a bunch of conflicts but I won't tell you about them!

• Are you a Certified Financial Planner practitioner?

◇ Great answer: Yes!

◇ Not great answer: "What does that mean?"

• Can you give me a reference from someone with a similar situation to mine?

◇ Great answer: Yes!

◇ Not great answers: "No, you are my first client."

And some some questions to ask yourself:

- Do you prefer to meet in an office or virtually? In-office meetings will facilitate a deeper relationship and allow everyone to read body language; virtual meetings will allow you to work with the best advisors across the country.
- Do you prefer someone your age or a different age? Perhaps a younger advisor will have a fresh perspective, an older advisor will have wisdom, or you may connect easier with someone your own age.
- Do you prefer to work with an advisor who is a "one-person band," someone with a small support team, or someone with a large support team? You may prefer the hands-on approach of a solo advisor; you may prefer a higher level of service from a support team; or you might value a larger firm that will have multiple advisors available for you.
- Does anyone you know work with an advisor they trust? Ask friends, family, or coworkers for an introduction.

What if there is no hope?

There is always hope! You can always pull one of the four levers. Regardless of your situation, any problem big or small can be improved by pulling the levers. Keep working where it's enjoyable, spend less money where possible, save more if you can, and take more risk if it makes sense. No matter how dire your situation is, it can always be improved. You can always take action to change your situation. These improvements, no matter how small, will improve the situation. Furthermore, making many small improvements will start to have a compounding effect where over time, the situation may become drastically improved. There can be a "snowball" effect to making change. Start small, then add to it, then add again and again. It will take time and it may be difficult, but the changes will make an impact.

Start With Why, a book written by Simon Sinek, gives us another clue (and classic hallmark of a good book) by giving us the most important information right in the title. *Start with why*. Making changes in life is difficult in any area: personal finance, relationships, health, fitness, and diet. And the fact that these are all related is an idea for a different book! It's helpful to start with "why?" Why are you making these changes? Why are they important to you? Why is this temporary pain worth it in the long run? Why now? Why do you wish to retire? Why do you wish to improve your financial situation? Answering these questions will help define your motivations and why these changes are important to you. And there are no wrong answers! But the answers to the question of "why" need to be compelling enough to keep you motivated and on track during difficult times. Then keep these motivations in mind as the pain from change starts. And it always does because change is always painful. But over time the difficulty will subside, and the improvements will remain. This is how to improve any situation!

"Where the determination is, the way can be found."
–*The Richest Man in Babylon* by George S. Clason

Appendix A – Budget worksheet

My income this month

Income	Monthly total
Paychecks (salary after taxes, benefits, and check cashing fees)	$
Other income (after taxes) for example: child support	$
Total monthly income	$ 0.00

Income

My expenses this month

	Expenses	Monthly total
HOUSING	Rent or mortgage	$
	Renter's insurance or homeowner's insurance	$
	Utilities (like electricity and gas)	$
	Internet, cable, and phones	$
	Other housing expenses (like property taxes)	$
FOOD	Groceries and household supplies	$
	Meals out	$
	Other food expenses	$
TRANSPORTATION	Public transportation and taxis	$
	Gas for car	$
	Parking and tolls	$
	Car maintenance (like oil changes)	$
	Car insurance	$
	Car loan	$
	Other transportation expenses	$

Appendix A – Budget worksheet

	Expenses	Monthly total
HEALTH	Medicine	$
	Health insurance	$
	Other health expenses (like doctors' appointments and eyeglasses)	$
PERSONAL AND FAMILY	Child care	$
	Child support	$
	Money given or sent to family	$
	Clothing and shoes	$
	Laundry	$
	Donations	$
	Entertainment (like movies and amusement parks)	$
	Other personal or family expenses (like beauty care)	$
FINANCE	Fees for cashier's checks and money transfers	$
	Prepaid cards and phone cards	$
	Bank or credit card fees	$
	Other fees	$
OTHER	School costs (like supplies, tuition, student loans)	$
	Other payments (like credit cards and savings)	$
	Other expenses this month	$
	Total monthly expenses	$ 0.00

Expenses

Appendix B – savings priorities

Congratulations, after paying all your bills each month, you have money left over to save. This book has discussed a plethora of ways to save for retirement. What to do first?!

Priority	What to do with your money
1	Make sure you have a decent health plan covering loved ones who might depend on you with a deductible you can manage.
2	Set aside at least three months of expenses in a cash reserve. If you have a mortgage, consider setting aside six months of expenses. Ensure you can cover your health insurance deductible.
3	Save to your employer's retirement plan up to the match. This is free money!
4	If you meet the limitations, save to a Roth IRA.
5	If one is available, save to an HSA.
6	Save to your employer's retirement plan up to the maximum amount, including catch-up if 50 or older.
7	If your employer has a 401(k), investigate if after-tax contributions are an option.
8	If you have some need for life insurance, establish a permanent life insurance policy and save to the cash value.
9	Save to a non-qualified annuity.
10	If you've done all these things and there is still cash to invest, congratulations! Seek alternative investments.

References

1. Caporal, J. (2021, May 26). *Average Retirement Savings in the U.S.: $65,000*. The Motley Fool. https://www.fool.com/research/average-retirement-savings/

2. CDC. (2022, August 31). *Life Expectancy in the U.S. Dropped for the Second Year in a Row in 2021*. Www.cdc.gov. https://www.cdc.gov/nchs/pressroom/nchs_press_releases/2022/20220831.htm

3. Bureau, U. C. (n.d.). *Around the World, Living Longer and Healthier Depends Largely on Gender and Countries' Income*. Census.gov. https://www.census.gov/library/stories/2021/05/long-life-does-not-always-mean-a-healthy-life-in-old-age.html

4. National Air and Space Museum. (2019). *Roll, Pitch, and Yaw | How Things Fly*. Si.edu. https://howthingsfly.si.edu/flight-dynamics/roll-pitch-and-yaw

5. "Providence starts year with 162 teacher vacancies" www.wpri.com, Aug 29, 2022; "School districts look overseas to fill teacher shortages" www.edweek.org, Oct 21, 2022; "Biden, job search companies partner to take on teacher shortages" www.usatoday.com, Aug 31, 2022.

6. "Virtual mentoring: what is it, and how to build an effective online mentorship program," www.wildapricot.com, April 14, 2022.

7. Gravier, E. (2021, April 6). *Here are the best free budgeting tools of 2021*. CNBC. https://www.cnbc.com/select/best-free-budgeting-tools/

8. Prosperous Retirement: Guide to the New Reality, Michael Stein, pages 16-18.

9. Team, Usaf. D. P. (2023, April 25). *Half of American households have no retirement savings*. USAFacts. https://usafacts.org/data-projects/retirement-savings

10. Bureau, U. C. (2022, January 13). *Those Who Married Once More Likely Than Others to Have Retirement Savings*. Census.gov.

References

https://www.census.gov/library/stories/2022/01/women-more-likely-than-men-to-have-no-retirement-savings.html

11. *67 percent of private industry workers had access to retirement plans in 2020 : The Economics Daily: U.S. Bureau of Labor Statistics*. (n.d.). Www.bls.gov. https://www.bls.gov/opub/ted/2021/67-percent-of-private-industry-workers-had-access-to-retirement-plans-in-2020.htm

12. *Riversource Tax Control Guide*. (n.d.). Www.riversource.com. Retrieved October 14, 2023, from https://www.riversource.com/spotlight/teriguide/

13. Bureau, U. C. (n.d.). *New Data Reveal Inequality in Retirement Account Ownership*. Census.gov. https://www.census.gov/library/stories/2022/08/who-has-retirement-accounts.html

14. *Make a Budget*. (n.d.). https://consumer.gov/sites/default/files/pdf-1020-make-budget-worksheet_form.pdf